Becoming a
Rainmaker

Becoming a Rainmaker

Creating a Downpour of Serious Money

By Matt Oechsli

Total Achievement Publishing
P.O. Box 29385
Greensboro, NC 27429

First edition.

Designed and typeset by Sans Serif Inc., Saline, MI
Cover design by KCL Creative, Ramseur, NC
Printed in the United States of America

ISBN: 0-9656765-7-9

Contents

Introduction   1

Section I   Rainmakers Are Made, Not Born   3
    Chapter 1   The Brass Ring   5
    Chapter 2   The Rich Are Different   20

Section II   The Rainmaker Mindset   29
    Chapter 3   A Matter of Mindset   31
    Chapter 4   Developing the Mindset of a Warrior   44

Section III   The Activities of a Rainmaker   53
    Chapter 5   Common Sense, But Not Common Practice   55
    Chapter 6   Maximize High Impact Activities   70
    Chapter 7   Minimize Low Impact Activities   90

Section IV   The Right Skills   103
    Chapter 8   Handling the Face-to-Face   105
    Chapter 9   Refine Your Rainmaking Skills   116
    Chapter 10   Use the Web (Your Prospects Do)   127
    Chapter 11   Psych Yourself Up, Not Out   136
    Chapter 12   The 12 Commandments of Rainmaking   144

Section V   The Rainmaker Critical Path System   157

About the Author   167
Index   168

Introduction

The secret of success of every man [or woman] who has ever been successful lies in the fact that he [or she] formed the habit of doing things that failures don't like to do.

—Albert E. N. Gray
1940 National Association of Life Underwriters Convention

I nearly called this book, "Back to Basics—with a 21st Century Reality Check," because the principles that I've outlined are timeless. By combining our most recent research on Rainmakers (who they are, what do they do, what sets them apart) with 25 years of professional coaching experience, I have designed a blueprint for becoming a Rainmaker. If you're already a Rainmaker—congratulations! Your next objective is to become a Master Rainmaker.

Rainmakers are a rare breed. They are self-sufficient, make lots of money, reward themselves handsomely for their efforts, and they're extremely proud of their prowess. Rainmakers are the engines that produce new business. But you can't hire one. You have to become one.

It sometimes seems that everyone on Earth is marketing products and services to the affluent. But marketing is one thing; selling is another. Our research reveals that very few financial professionals are Rainmakers. By our definition, a Rainmaker acquires at least 10 clients, worth upwards of a million dollars, every 12 months. That seems simple enough—until you consider that only 7% of the financial professionals surveyed actually made those numbers.

This is why I've written this book. We now have empirical data that's enabled us to develop a *statistically significant* profile of the 21st

Century Rainmaker. I'm a zealous advocate of higher education and continuous learning, but by replicating this profile, you can attain personal affluence much faster than you could with any degree or professional designation.

I have presented the Rainmaker profile as a three-legged stool, because each leg represents a critical component of becoming a true Rainmaker. The first leg represents the *Mindset* of a Rainmaker. We know how they think, the risks they take, their level of commitment and much more. Many people buy into the myth that you're either born with the right mindset, or you're not. This is completely false. At the Oechsli Institute, we have bred many Rainmakers who were born without the proper mindset.

The second leg is *High-Impact Activities.* We know what works, which activities produce only medium impact, and which are a waste of your time, money and energy. My objective is to help you perform these high-impact activities as a matter of habit. These activities are simple, but not necessarily easy.

Finally, we have the third leg of the Rainmaker stool—skills. We've discovered that Rainmakers are both subtle and direct. They practice sales skills that are so seamless, they are nearly invisible. In addition, Rainmakers apply specific do's and don'ts to achieve their goals—e.g., obtaining introductions and asking for referrals. With a little knowledge and consistent practice, the Rainmaker's skills are easy to master.

The following chapters will teach you how to think like a Rainmaker, perform the activities of a Rainmaker, and master the skills of a Rainmaker.

Leave your comfort zone behind! Go for it! Become a true Rainmaker!

Matt Oechsli

SECTION I

Rainmakers Are Made, Not Born

1

The Brass Ring

Although 95% of financial advisors target the affluent, only 7% acquired 10+ clients with assets of at least $1 million in the previous year.

— Factoid, 2005 ANAC Research*

What does it take to become a Rainmaker?

What custom blend of personal magnetism, skill, discipline and savvy is needed to acquire at least 10 affluent clients every year—people with investable assets exceeding $250,000 (and preferably $1 million)? According to recent estimates, more than 17 million U.S. households earn annual incomes topping $100,000. What's more, high-income households are projected to grow at a faster rate than households in general. And these affluent households spend plenty of money—on everything from vacation homes, boats and luxury cars to high-end financial and legal services. Never before have there been so many opportunities to become affluent by serving the affluent.

Are you landing your share of these clients?

Most service professionals aren't, but not for lack of trying.

Based on our 2005 ANAC Research, for example, 95% of financial advisors target prospects with at least $250,000 in investable assets. Ninety-five percent! In fact, of the 819 financial advisors responding to

---

* ANAC Research refers to the 2004–2005 research project *Attracting New Affluent Clients,* commissioned by the Oechsli Institute. A factoid is a brief fact taken from that research.

our survey, most were very clear about the asset level they target, and the minimum level they'll accept from a new client. Their efforts to capture affluent clients are written into business plans and incorporated into training programs. For some professionals, becoming a Rainmaker is akin to finding the Holy Grail.

Chart 1	
Survey Respondents Who Added 10+ New Clients	
Targeted Investable Asset Level	**Added 10+ New Clients**
$1 million and higher	7%
$500,000 to $1 million	12%
$250,000 to $500,000	26%

Why are only 7% of the financial advisors targeting clients with $1 million or more in investable assets able to "grab the brass ring?"[1]

Is it that "many are called, but few are chosen?" No! In truth, many are called, but few choose to *do what it takes*. Almost anyone willing to *do what it takes* can become a Rainmaker. This is truly an equal opportunity career.

Rainmaker vs. Wannabe

To illustrate the difference between a true Rainmaker and a Rainmaker wannabe, I'd like to share the stories of two financial advisors. Both are veterans; both know what they need to do; both are successful (one far more so), and both are targeting the affluent.

Peter[2] is a Rainmaker. Although he seemed to possess the proper mindset before he entered into a coaching relationship with the Oechsli Institute, our mission was to raise his game by strengthening his mindset, helping him meet higher-level prospects and refining his

---

[1] This figure may be as low as 2%. The survey's margin of error was plus or minus 5%. We chose to use the highest figure of 7%.

[2] Throughout this book, I've assigned pseudonyms to the people mentioned in my case histories.

skills. The first step in strengthening his mindset was to define his ideal (affluent) prospect and determine an annual goal for the coming year. This was fairly easy. He wanted 15+ new relationships worth more than $1 million in investable assets, which (by his estimate) would translate into $150,000–$250,000 in additional annual fees. Several months into our coaching, I had a conversation with Peter that illustrates what sets Rainmakers apart from the crowd.

Peter: "I've already brought in seven new ideal affluent relationships, but it's been extremely frustrating. It's so slow. I'm in front of the right people, but I have to be so careful orchestrating the right windows of opportunity that sometimes I think I'm spinning my wheels.

"A perfect example is a large dinner function tonight. We're celebrating a new wing at the hospital. The 'who's who' in the community will be there, but it's not the kind of event where you can talk business. However, just for you, I'm attending. But I've got to tell you, you and your high-impact Rainmaker activities are a pain in my ass!"

Matt: "Wow! You sound like a whining Rainmaker wannabe."

Peter: "What did you just call me?"

Matt: "You heard me. You're whining—complaining about doing your high-impact activities, which is exactly what Rainmaker wannabes do. Here's a question. How many people are going to be at this dinner, and how many qualify for your ideal affluent profile?"

Peter: "There will be about 50 people there, and they all qualify. But Matt, you're not listening to me. It will not be acceptable to discuss business."

Matt: "I'm listening. How many of those 50 people know you, like you, and respect you as a professional?"

Peter: "They'd all better! Heck, I chaired the committee that raised the money to build this wing, and two of the most respected doctors at the hospital are long-term clients who served on this committee with me."

Matt: "If that's true, you're really being a wimp. Here's the drill. Are you ready?"

Peter: "I guess."

Matt: "Can you write down the names of four people attending that you'd love to have as clients?"

Peter: "Sure."

Matt: "OK. Write down their names, and here's your mission. During the course of this dinner, subtly approach each of these people, one at a time, and whisper some version of 'I want to put my professional hat on and roll a couple of things by you next week. Can you grab breakfast on Wednesday?'

Peter: "No wonder why I pay you guys the big bucks. I can do that! I guess I was whining."

Matt: "No harm, no foul. Call me on my cell phone tomorrow, and let me know how things went."

How many affluent prospects did Peter place in the pipeline that night? If you guessed four, you're wrong. It was six, because when Peter arrived at the dinner, he immediately saw two others he wanted to approach. But that wouldn't have happened if he hadn't already possessed the mindset of a Rainmaker. For some reason, Peter was having a bad day when he called me. He was doing the right rainmaker activities and possessed the right mindset. All he needed was a gentle push in the right direction.

Peter had already laid much of the groundwork. He'd made the effort over the previous months to build relationships with these six individuals. It was on this basis that he could approach them on a business level with the subtle assertiveness of a Rainmaker. Before you arrive at Peter's stage, of being able to transform a non-business relationship into a business relationship, the individuals you want to approach must get to know you, determine whether or not they like you, and develop clear reasons to trust you on a personal level. It's simple, but not easy.

Now, let's meet Greg.

Greg very much wants to be a Rainmaker. We'd discussed it several times before Greg informed me that he'd recently attended a family wedding. The event occurred at a beautiful resort, and lasted three days. The facilities were so luxurious that most guests were delighted to spend all three days on site. Greg engaged in numerous conversations that provided openings to talk about his professional expertise. Because Greg is so soft-spoken and trustworthy, people naturally open up to him. What an advantage!

Not wanting to appear pushy, and assuming he was in no position to compete for their business, Greg tended to talk about his business in general terms—and actually felt relieved when people changed the subject! A couple of times, he sensed that the person with whom he was talking might be interested in his services, so he handed out his business card, and invited the person to call.

As Greg was flying home, he found himself replaying many of the conversations from those three days. As he did, he remembered several openings he could have (and should have!) boldly exploited. When we talked later, he readily admitted that he'd blown a golden Rainmaking opportunity.

The McClellan Mindset

History is replete with stories of people who resisted capitalizing on the opportunities before them. General George C. McClellan, who was given command of the Army of the Potomac in November 1861, was a famous practitioner of procrastination and the "can't do" philosophy. A master of discipline and drill, the "young Napoleon" was overly cautious—to the point of paranoia—about pitting his numerically superior armies against those of Confederate generals Joseph Johnston and Robert E. Lee. McClellan frequently exaggerated the enemy's strength and his own logistical problems to excuse his lack of initiative. At one point, after Abraham Lincoln had spent months begging him to attack, McClellan suggested that Lincoln should come do the job himself if he thought it was so easy to beat the rebels. Needless to say, McClellan was neither in uniform nor anywhere near Appomattox when the Civil War came to a close.

I'm not a forensic psychologist, but it's clear to me that McClellan was suffering from a condition that afflicts many would-be Rainmakers—fear! The fear of failure, fear of rejection, fear of a bruised ego, fear of feeling self-conscious among wealthy people traveling in the "elite circles" of country clubs, charitable foundations and powerful civic associations. I'll discuss how to overcome such fears in later chapters, but for now, suffice it to say that true Rainmakers learn to play through their fears. As one client recently said, "I felt the fear, but plowed ahead anyway."

To become a Rainmaker, you must "work without a net." The "net" is any excuse, any rationalization, any form of procrastination used to cushion the ego from a potential blow. Maybe you're familiar with some of the excuses—everything from "the new brochures aren't ready" and "I'm too busy managing existing accounts" to "I don't want to come off like a cheap salesman."

Fear is toxic to the Rainmaker mindset. If you allow it to dominate your thinking, you'll never get the bat off your shoulder.

The Right Mindset

According to our research, three factors are critical to becoming a Rainmaker:

1. Your mindset—the way you *think*
2. Your activities—what you *do*; and
3. Your skills—*how* you prospect.

What's interesting is how much Rainmakers have in common with Tiger Woods. When Tiger won the 2005 British Open, his tenth major victory in 35 attempts (Jack Nicklaus won 18 majors in over 180 attempts), reporters interviewed his swing coach, Hank Haney, to learn what it was like to coach the best golfer in the world. After all, Tiger was already ranked #1 in the world when he hired Hank Haney to replace Butch Harmon, who had coached him to such a high level of success. What was it like to coach the best golfer? How do you coach Tiger Woods? What sets Tiger apart from other golfers you've coached?

Haney said it was a coach's dream to work with Tiger Woods. Essentially, he said, "There are three things that set Tiger Woods apart:

- He is <u>always</u> looking to improve his game.
- Tiger is <u>fearless</u>, takes risks, and is not afraid to fail (he plays without a net).
- Tiger Woods is the <u>hardest worker</u> on the tour.

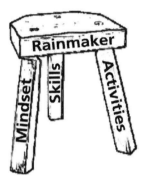

These three qualities, which set Tiger Woods apart from all other professional golfers, are the same qualities that differentiate Peter from Greg and the other wannabes. Peter is fearless. He's set big goals, and is totally committed to going after them. Rainmakers are always refining their sales skills, always looking to improve. They work both hard and smart, engaging in high-impact activities even when they might rather be doing something else. Peter knew he had to attend this dinner; he simply needed a gentle reminder to work smart.

These factors comprise the three legs of the Rainmaking stool. No one leg, or pair of legs, is sufficient to become a Rainmaker—to ensure that you will acquire 10 or more affluent clients each year. And no component can be implemented without the others. You can't acquire the proper mindset *before* refining your skills *before* engaging in the right activities. There's no "egg comes before the chicken" here. Every leg must be fitted simultaneously or the stool will tip over. On the plus side, once you commit to improving any single element—mindset, activities or skills—you can't help but make progress with the other two parts of the equation.

Everything a Rainmaker does is linked to (and pulled toward) a clear purpose—landing 10+ new affluent clients. From here, the Rainmaker sets specific long-term and short-term goals, which color and shape her approach to every prospecting activity and event. The Rainmaker knows how many people she wants to connect with, and she has a list of specific individuals in her sights at all times.

That's where the mindset begins, and that's the first reason Greg failed to capitalize on his opportunity. Although Greg knew a golden opportunity was unfolding, he had no clarity of purpose, no objectives and no action plan when he left for that wedding. He was also unwilling to work without a net—to take risks, be fearless, and not be afraid to fail.

The contrast with Peter is obvious. Already a Rainmaker in both mindset and activities, he was refining his skills to make certain he could take full advantage of any opportunity. Clarity of purpose, translated into specific and measurable goals is what keeps Rainmakers focused. Peter attended the dinner function bent on putting affluent prospects into his pipeline. He cut through the distractions, and remained laser-focused on what he wanted to achieve. He was willing to take risks and enjoy the challenges of *working outside his comfort zone.*

The contrast with Greg is even more telling when placed in the context of the brief skill coaching session I had with Peter. Peter is committed to bringing in 15 new affluent clients. That's different from trying or hoping. He's also willing to work on his game. I noticed a flaw and gave him simple instructions. He accepted my coaching and ran with it. Peter played without a net, attended that dinner function, and executed his lessons beautifully under real-life circumstances. He was able to do that because he possesses the mindset of a warrior.

If Greg had been discussing this same event with me, and I offered the same skill coaching, he would not have executed. Why? Because that devilish little voice of doubt would have whispered in his ear, "You can't do that! Matt doesn't know what it's like at these functions." Greg would have listened to his fears, attended the dinner, observed the four prospects whose names he'd jotted down, and been too afraid to act.

This would have created cognitive dissonance, which could easily cause Greg to stop doing future high-impact Rainmaker activities. Ouch!

The Right Activities

To become a Rainmaker, replace the question, "What should I do today?" with "What *must* I do today to achieve my goals?" Your highest-priority activities must be *directly* related to developing personal relationships with affluent prospects. These are the *right* activities in the world of Rainmakers, and the right mindset enables Rainmakers to approach those activities eagerly and without hesitation.

Are you eager to engage in each of the following? You should be. These prospecting activities are the only ones that really matter:

- Locating affluent prospects.
- Getting face-to-face with new affluent prospects.
- Handling the first face-to-face meeting.
- Proving your competency to the affluent prospect.
- Closing the sale.

OK. These activities are not the *only ones* that matter, but they *are the highest-impact activities* in terms of lead conversion.

In the second quarter of 2004, we commissioned an independent study to determine how affluent consumers make major purchasing decisions. According to the APD Research,[3] when deciding *where* to look for options, survey respondents gave the highest credibility to opinions and suggestions from their immediate family and trusted friends. Our research and coaching experience confirms that affluent consumers *do not* respond well to direct mail and cold calling—among other things.

Seminars can be moderately successful when targeted to the right people. But the prospecting methods that produce the greatest impact are targeted networking, referrals and introductions. To succeed, these

---

[3] APD Research refers to *How the Affluent Make Purchasing Decisions*, commissioned by the Oechsli Institute, June 2004.

activities require that you develop strong personal relationships with both your affluent prospects and clients. And you do this by attending or arranging live, real-time, in-person encounters—as many as it takes. In many ways, it's like a romance: you have to been seen, let your target (prospect) get to know you, and then very carefully let your intentions become known.

You can't buy their business with slick brochures, websites or direct-mail campaigns. You don't land them with hype, vague value propositions or "platinum-level" packages. You won't get their business unless they see genuine value in what you have to offer. You have to provide Ritz-Carlton service with FedEx efficiency. You have to be the real deal. On a consistent basis, in a myriad of ways, you must be able to quantify, demonstrate, and communicate your value.

If you want to win business from the affluent, first win their confidence. *They must come to like you, trust you, and respect you as a professional—period!*

Unfortunately, our research shows that many professionals are reluctant to use high-impact prospecting activities. Among those reluctant to prospect, 50% said locating prospects was *extremely challenging,* and 52% were hesitant about face-to-face meetings. Is it any wonder that so many "big fish" are getting away?

Finding affluent prospects is an obstacle that Rainmakers quickly overcome. While developing the Rainmaker's mindset, they acquire the habit of activating their prospecting antenna for new ideal prospects. Field biologists refer to this as a *search engine.*

Martin is a perfect example of how this antenna functions. When I first met Martin to assist him in becoming a Rainmaker, one of his initial assignments was to make a Rainmaker Dream List of all the people (he knew of) that qualified as ideal clients, and who he would like to have as clients. In 48 hours, he could think of only five names. Three years later, after Martin had exceeded everyone's expectations in his Rainmaking abilities (he was bringing in over 80 million dollars in new assets a year), I was conducting a Rainmaker workshop for his firm. Martin attended, and when I reached the Rainmaker Dream List exercise, he had already written down the names of prospects he wanted to target. He'd listed a total of 62 names worth more than one billion dollars in assets! To make my point about his Rainmaking antenna, I asked Martin if he could recall how many names were on his first Rainmaker Dream List. His peers were shocked at the answer.

Rainmaker wannabes are reluctant to prospect. They engage in the sort of avoidance behavior exhibited by Greg. Helping Peter fine-tune his skills was easy, because he consistently conducted high-impact Rainmaking activities. Greg knew what to do, and how to do it, but he wasn't doing it. *My objective is to increase your awareness of what to do, refine your ability to do it, and ensure that you perform the right activities on a consistent basis.*

The Right Skills

Greg hesitated to grab opportunities staring him in the face because he assumed he was in no position to compete for the business. He even felt relieved when prospects changed the subject. In other words, he had zero confidence in his selling skills when he came face-to-face with people of wealth.

Rainmakers are skilled in selling to the affluent. For them, the process begins with "strategic intent"—with the objective of transforming a particular individual into a client—followed by subtle, "seamless" selling tactics that they apply for however long it takes. How do Rainmakers like Peter acquire these skills? Do they learn these skills in a classroom? Do they learn them before venturing into the world of the affluent, or do they build the skills along the way?

In my experience, Rainmakers engage in experiential learning— mastering the necessary skills while performing the right activities. They frequently learn how to do the right activities through trial and error. A common Rainmaker statement goes something like this: *"The only reason it might appear that I know what I'm doing is because I've made every mistake in the book."* Remember, Rainmakers are not afraid to fail; they play without a net.

Many financial advisors are paralyzed by preparation. They fear venturing out until they are skilled enough to avoid failure. They fear not having the proper tools—an adequate brochure, the reputation of an "expert," the right team infrastructure. In these cases, fear of failure is not what really stops them, but a simple failure to:

- Develop goals that articulate their desires, enabling them to look past fears, and concentrate on what they want to achieve.
- Select and perform the right high-impact activities to achieve their goals, which maintain their focus and keep them on the critical path.
- Engage in goal-driven activities that help them learn the right skills. Rainmakers continually refine their skills, because they are constantly engaging in the right activities.

The Name's Bond, James Bond

A popular misconception about the Rainmaker is that he's a born schmoozer—a charismatic James Bond who plays baccarat with countesses in the morning, shoots birdies with CEOs in the afternoon, and charms Hollywood starlets at gin-soaked soirees in the evening. In short, the biggest myth about Rainmakers is that they are super-socialites, networking gurus and Machiavellian politicians. Not true! I've met many a glad-hander and smooth talker, and very few are Rainmakers. Why? Because few know how to sell, and most are unwilling to leave their comfort zones, become disciplined, and consistently put business into the pipeline.

The true Rainmaker is less James Bond and more Columbo—the Peter Falk detective who was "dumb like a fox." The Rainmaker knows how to listen, learn and gather "intel" on prime prospects. He does his homework, conducts reconnaissance, and keeps his antennae tuned for any hint of opportunity. When the moment is right, he engages in face-to-face encounters, and applies selling skills that are so subtle (but not too subtle) and seamless that the object of his desire doesn't feel put upon. Instead, the affluent prospect—over the course of weeks, months or years—may well be the first to broach the subject of business.

Perks and Pitfalls

There are many obvious benefits to becoming a Rainmaker. Chief among them is dramatically increasing your firm's revenue—and your own income—with less time and effort than you'll need to recruit dozens (or hundreds) of less-affluent clients.

- *Financial advisors* who bring in 10+ new $1 million dollar clients generate $100,000 of new revenue—most, if not all, in the form of recurring fees. Of course, the picture grows even brighter if you establish 10 new client relationships with people investing $5 million or $10 million, which translates into $500,000 or $1,000,000 of additional revenue.
- *Certified Public Accountants* who land 10+ new affluent clients create $100,000, $250,000 or $500,000+ of new business for the firm.
- *Attorneys* who recruit 10 or more affluent clients can expect to increase billable hours by a significant percentage.

In addition, there are powerful, if less tangible, benefits to becoming a Rainmaker. One is the amazing boost to self-esteem and personal energy that comes from doing what you love, and doing it well. You'll enjoy a more optimistic, can-do attitude—a sense of empowerment and confidence that comes from being "out there"; being self-sufficient. The money and lifestyle are obvious advantages, but the increased feelings of self-worth, independence and optimism are just as important. The Rainmakers I've met are truly at peace with themselves and the world.

On the flip side, there is a real price to be paid for *not* becoming a Rainmaker, especially in the financial services and legal fields— professions that breed many Rainmakers. Chronic underachievement acts as a cancer on self-esteem and self-confidence, causing some people to become cynical and pessimistic. They habitually extend the wrong antennae, and then compile lists of why they haven't succeeded, why the right mindset, skills and activities don't work. Worse, they become jealous and resentful of Rainmakers in order to justify their underperformance. They assume that Rainmakers lie and cheat to coax people into doing business. Jealousy is an ugly emotion that is often found in Rainmaker wannabes.

Worst of all, they lose their ability to dream. They lose their faith. They deactivate their instinctive achievement cycle, which dictates that you must set a goal and do what's necessary until the goal is reached. Having lost goal-focus, they totally disengage from the achievement cycle, and become trapped within the confines of their comfort zone. You probably know such people, but I have every confidence that you'll never become one of them.

There's nothing complicated about becoming a Rainmaker, though many people (consultants and coaches—to name a few) make it seem complicated. On the other hand, there are no short-cuts or silver bullets either. You become a Rainmaker by developing relationships with affluent clients. You win their friendship, trust and professional respect. Once this is accomplished, these "centers-of-influence" will likely provide you with a stream of introductions and referrals. To get started, you simply need to adjust your mindset, skills and activities. From there, you need merely to maintain your focus, your energy levels and your persistence to keep the ball rolling.

SUMMARY

Although 95% of respondents to the ANAC Survey target the most affluent prospects, only 7% acquired at least 10 clients with investable assets exceeding $1 million in the previous year. Becoming a Rainmaker is a matter of simultaneously developing the proper mindset, skills and activities through experiential learning—i.e., on-the-job training. Most important, the true Rainmaker focuses almost exclusively on high-impact prospecting activities, which include obtaining personal referrals, introductions and face-to-face meetings. The benefits of becoming a Rainmaker are both financial and emotional, as are the costs of not becoming one.

Research Facts

▶ Only 12% of ANAC Survey respondents acquired clients with investable assets of $500,000 to $1 million in the previous year, while 26% brought in clients with assets of $250,000 to $500,000.

▶ According to our APD Research on how affluent consumers make purchasing decisions, networking, referrals and introductions represent the highest-impact prospecting activities.

▶ Significant numbers of financial advisors are reluctant to conduct high-impact prospecting activities.

▶ The three factors critical to becoming a Rainmaker are mindset, activities and skills.

TAKING ACTION

- Be honest with yourself. A true Rainmaker, or Rainmaker in training, never lies to himself/herself.
- Make a commitment right now to start down the path toward becoming a Rainmaker. For starters, it couldn't hurt to continue reading this book.
- Use the 3-legged Rainmaker Stool and write out *one thing* you want to learn, master, or improve per leg.

2

The Rich Are Different

When making a major purchase decision, affluent consumers ranked price as the least important criteria.
— Factoid, 2004 APD Research

My chapter title isn't meant to suggest that the affluent are a different species of homo sapiens—an enigmatic breed of bluebloods worthy of fear, fascination and envy. On the other hand, don't believe for a New York minute that wealthy consumers are simply Average Joes with money to burn. Most of your target clients don't fit either the Thurston Howell III or Beverly Hillbillies stereotypes. Unfortunately, many service professionals seem to base their sales and service approach on these tired clichés.

Selling to the affluent begins, logically enough, with getting to know the affluent. So let's take a quick course in how the affluent think. How do they make spending decisions? What kinds of research do they perform? If price isn't the chief criterion in making purchase decisions, what is? What must you do to win their loyalty and repeat business?

Let's take a peek into the affluent mind.[4]

First of all, most have *not* inherited their wealth. And few are cloistered in exclusive enclaves, unwilling to associate with the "little people." Instead, many have emerged from middle-class backgrounds to

---

[4] For a more thorough discussion, please see my previous book, *The Art of Selling to the Affluent*, John Wiley & Sons. Hoboken, NJ: 2005.

become generators and earners of wealth. In all likelihood, your afflu-ent prospect is a self-made man or woman.

Our 2004 APD Research determined that 22.4 % are business own-ers, 25.9% are self-employed professionals, and 44.9% are high-paid executives and commissioned employees (salespeople). Respondents were widely distributed across the six major geographical regions of the United States; 82% were between ages 35 and 64, with 11% under 35; 82.2% were male, and 17.8% female. Hard-working and entrepre-neurial, these affluent consumers are goal-focused, committed to their careers, and willing to pay the price for achievement. That price often takes the form of stress.

More than 75% of affluent business owners and self-employed professionals work over 60 hours per week. They never have enough time to finish their work, so when making a purchase decision, they ex-pect minimal hassles and maximum attention. Seven qualities associ-ated with making major purchase decisions were analyzed in terms of importance. Here's what we found:

- Two criteria stood above the rest: 83.3% said that offering the right set of features was very important; 75.8% said that being able to find the best possible option through careful evaluation and comparison was very important.
- 65.5% said that the opinions of immediate family members and trusted friends had a very significant impact on deciding where to look when making a major purchase decision, but only 37.8% said those opinions had a very significant impact on the final purchase decision.
- Once the search process is underway, the affluent place more confidence in their own ability to find information, sort through options, and make the final decision. Respondents also indicated that the Internet and trusted periodicals serve as major research vehicles.
- When given an opportunity to write in other criteria important to making major purchase decisions, warranties and guarantees won by a wide margin.

- Even though respondents were extremely price-value conscious, finding a discounted or sale price was not as critical to their final decision as expected.
- Problem resolution and post-purchase service rated as having the greatest impact on repeat business. Offering the lowest price ranked last.
- Respondents gave far less importance to reviews and testimonials than they did to the responsiveness of sales and service people.[5]

So, when all the statistics are analyzed, how are the rich different?

First of all, as you just discovered, approximately 93% are self-made. They are CEOs, upper management, large and small business owners, self-employed professionals, partners in professional practices (doctors, CPAs, etc.), and successful high-commissioned salespeople (Rainmakers). Although they tend to be hard chargers and consider themselves successful, as a rule they don't consider themselves "rich." Because of their drive and work ethic, however, they not only earn much more money than most people (a significant difference), they have three times the amount of stress. Thus, they don't like their precious time wasted, and they don't suffer fools. All these factors have contributed to their evolution as *extremely* discriminating consumers. The rich are different all right—they are looking for a servant. Don't laugh, because if you learn how to master this concept as a Rainmaker, you will quickly become affluent.

Life after the Sale

Selling to the affluent goes well beyond making the sale—although you *do* have to make the sale. It requires that you solve any problems quickly and satisfactorily, and deliver superior service following the purchase. Harold and Maude offer a perfect illustration of this point.

After building a nest egg worth more than $250,000, Harold—a home-based business owner—and his wife Maude pursued their

---

[5] From *The Art of Selling to the Affluent.*

dream of living in the country. They left a rent-stabilized apartment in New York City, and purchased a house on Maryland's rural Eastern Shore. Life looked like "Green Acres"—until tax time arrived.

Normally, Harold filed the family's tax returns using a popular software package. Because of the sheer volume of 2003 financial transactions (related to the move and a recent inheritance), Harold thought it wise to hire an accountant. He queried his mother-in-law, who lived nearby, as well as several neighbors for a referral. One name popped up again and again—that of John.

Harold telephoned John, and was greeted with a warm hello and greetings to all those who'd referred him. At their first meeting, John impressed Harold with his requests for detailed information and the fact that he prepared returns for the town's most prominent families. Harold was sold.

Six weeks after handing over his financial data, Harold hadn't heard anything from John. Two telephone messages went unanswered. Eight weeks later, John finally called to inform Harold that the returns were ready. Harold picked up the returns, wrote a check to John, and discussed possible future assignments. However, when Maude arrived home that evening, she discovered that John had failed to prepare a New York State and City return. Harold called to complain, but hung up when he was connected to voicemail. That night, he bought a copy of Turbo-Tax, and prepared the missing returns himself.

After April 15, John placed a "courtesy call" to Harold, who gave him a polite earful. John's reaction? He apologized for his egregious error, but suggested that—in the future—Harold prepare his own returns using Turbo-Tax!

You might think Harold acted a bit hastily by not giving John a chance to correct his mistake, and by paying for services not rendered. In fact, Harold's behavior was typical of affluent consumers—he demanded that the job be done quickly, correctly and with a minimum of fuss. When it became obvious that he'd "picked the wrong horse," he wasn't about to waste more valuable time, so he finished "the race" himself. Like many self-made men and women, Harold had neither the time nor the patience for shoddy service.

Value Trumps Price

Like many affluent clients, Harold cared less about price than the perceived value he received. When it comes to hiring financial advisors, accountants and attorneys, for example, value translates into prompt, courteous and efficient service. It also means solving problems rapidly, with minimal inconvenience to the client. Most important, it means *demonstrating* that you really care—not just saying you care. The following is a dramatic, but by no means unique, example.[6]

Imagine investing $5 million through a financial advisor. Three years later, your nest egg has dwindled to $2.5 million. That's what happened to Carol, and as you might expect, she was looking for a new financial advisor. Through someone in her church, she was referred to Jack, a fellow parishioner.

On the surface, this might appear to be a fairly simple case. Client has money; client loses 50% following the advice of someone she paid to provide such advice; dissatisfaction reaches a boiling point; client actively searches for an alternative. This should have been an easy sell for Jack, but he nearly blew it.

Jack saw immediately that the investments recommended by Carol's former advisor were selected for their healthy fees, not their suitability. He assumed that this was the problem, and launched into his typical risk-tolerance and asset-allocation pitch. "It finally dawned on me that I was losing her when her eyes started glazing over," he later told me. Out of desperation, he asked an obvious question: "Why are you dissatisfied with your financial advisor?" Expecting to hear a tale of woe about her lost millions, he was shocked when Carol instead talked about being passed off to the advisor's son while the advisor vacationed in Barbados. After Jack recounted the story, he said, "You know, not once did she complain about her losses."

Was this a bizarre anomaly? Perhaps. But selling to the affluent is full of anomalies. What the affluent have in common is that they earn

---

[6] Ibid.

more, have more cash to spend, and will pay you more in commissions and fees to get what they want. For those of you who understand how the affluent think, they are your treasure chest.

The state of customer service in this country has deteriorated to the point where many consumers expect (and accept) poor treatment. *Caveat Emptor* rules the land. For this reason, many people are happy when a business merely honors its promises—never mind exceeding expectations. But this doesn't apply to the affluent: they demand nothing less than superior service, attention to detail, and hassle-free problem resolution. The average person may be willing to spend hours on your customer-service or tech-support hotline. The affluent will refuse to dial the number. Yes, the affluent are the exception to typical consumer behavior, but they're the exception that proves the rule—for Rainmakers.

SUMMARY

Our 2004 APD Research indicates that most affluent prospects have not inherited their money, but have risen from middle-class backgrounds to become generators and earners of significant wealth. Your affluent prospect is probably a first-generation self-made man or woman. Before making a major purchase, affluent consumers conduct careful research to locate the right features and options, warranties and guarantees, and the most value for the price. As business owners or highly-paid professionals, these clients work long hours, and do not suffer fools lightly. They demand good service and rapid resolution of any problems that crop up.

Research Facts

▶ When making a major purchase decision, affluent consumers ranked price as the least important of seven different criteria.

▶ Of all APD respondents, 22.4 % are business owners, 25.9% are self-employed professionals, and 44.9% are high-paid executives and commissioned employees.

▶ More than 75% of affluent business owners and self-employed professionals surveyed work 60+ hours each week.

▶ 83.3% of APD respondents said offering the right features was very important to making a major purchase; 75.8% said that being able to find the best possible option through careful evaluation and comparison was very important.

▶ Of our APD respondents, 65.5% said the opinions of family members and friends had a very significant impact on deciding where to look when making a major purchase decision, but only 37.8% said those opinions had a very significant impact on the *final* decision.

TAKING ACTION

• Review your sales literature and website to determine where you need to personalize information in order to differentiate your value and help affluent consumers make a sound purchase decision.

• Make certain you can speak expertly and intelligibly about the products and services that you offer.

• Study your competitors to determine which products and options may give you the upper hand when it comes to attracting *and* retaining affluent clients.

- Review your current and past client list, and identify your top 25 clients. Then determine what sets them apart from everyone else. How did you get their business? How did you satisfy their needs and wants? Who introduced you to new prospects and why? How would they articulate your value—what you do?
- Coordinate your sales efforts with the efforts of your support and customer-service staff to ensure everyone provides the highest quality service, and works together to quickly resolve problems.

The Rainmaker Mindset

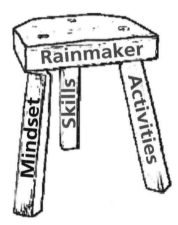

3

A Matter of Mindset

*Of the financial advisors who are eager to prospect, only 11%
said "finding prospects" was their most challenging prospecting activity.*

— Factoid, 2005 ANAC Research

The philosopher René Descartes famously said, "I think, therefore I
am," to repudiate the notion that human beings might be the figments
of some all-powerful demon's imagination.

Descartes' statement strikes me as ironic, because people often use
their own imaginations to conjure up all-powerful demons—to convince themselves that emotions are facts; impressions are reality; that
something can or can't be done. Mindset helps determine matter.

When you believe a task is easy, it's easy. When you think something will be difficult, it becomes difficult. When you're eager to perform an activity, you enjoy it. When you're reluctant to perform that
activity, you avoid it. Experiences and emotions shape your mindset,
which influence your behavior, which guides your actions.

Our 2005 ANAC Research divided financial advisors into two
camps—those eager to prospect and those reluctant to prospect. Financial advisors who were reluctant to prospect were likely to describe
high-impact activities as *extremely challenging*. Only a handful of those
eager to prospect agreed with that statement. Needless to say, the financial advisors who were reluctant to use high-impact methods were also
less likely to acquire new affluent clients. Mindset really does matter.

Chart 2		
The Percent of Survey Respondents Who Found a Prospecting Activity Extremely Challenging		
Prospecting Activity	EAGER to Prospect	RELUCTANT to Prospect
Finding Prospects	11%	50%
Introductions and Referrals	1%	26%
Getting Face-to-Face	1%	52%
Handling the First Face-to-Face Meeting	0%	11%
Proving Competency to a Prospect	0%	13%
Closing the Sale	0%	19%

I recognize that Chart 2 (above) outlines a series of prospecting activities, and that this section and chapter are about Mindset. But take a moment to carefully study this chart. Notice the high percentage of survey respondents who were reluctant to "find prospects" and engage in "getting face-to-face." Both of these activities are essential prerequisites to all the others. Whether or not they do occur is primarily a Mindset issue.

Let's face it: nothing is easy—at first. Learning to walk isn't easy, and neither is learning to read, write, add, subtract or drive a car. Given practice, however, these feats become routine. It takes repeated application of specific skills and activities to develop the mindset that says, "This task is easy."

The same principle applies to developing the Rainmaker mindset. You must repeatedly employ particular skills and activities to fine-tune the Rainmaker mindset—and trial and error is part of the process. Do you already have the mindset of a Rainmaker? Take this quick assessment to help answer that question.

Chart 3		
Rainmaker Mindset Self-Assessment		
Circle YES or NO for each question		
1. Do you have specific and measurable long-range and short-range goals?	Yes	No
2. Do you have specific 12-month Rainmaking targets (a specific number of new $1 million clients)?	Yes	No
3. Do you cut through all distractions and stay focused on what you want to achieve?	Yes	No
4. Are you willing to take risks and step outside your comfort zone?	Yes	No
5. Are you always looking for opportunities to prospect for affluent clients?	Yes	No
6. Are you flexible, able to adjust quickly and capitalize on new affluent prospect opportunities?	Yes	No
7. Do you have a specific profile of your ideal prospect?	Yes	No
8. Do Rainmaking opportunities seem to come your way naturally?	Yes	No
9. Are you obsessed with your Rainmaking goals?	Yes	No
10. Do you love Rainmaking?	Yes	No

Don't be alarmed if you scored a lot of No's. It's very common at this stage. Your mission is to be brutally honest with yourself and ask "Why?" for each "No." Then determine (with the help of this book) the actions you need to take to transform each No into a Yes.

The Rainmaker Game Plan

A select group of financial and legal services professionals bring in 10 or more $1 million relationships every year. Peter will bring in 15. You can do the same. The game begins when you commit to high-impact activities, and continually perfect your skills. It begins when you commit to the Rainmaker Game Plan, which is summarized below:

Mindset

- Learn to "play without a net."
- Select your target customer based on asset or income thresholds.
- Commit to bringing in "X" number of new clients in 12 months.
- Cut through distractions and stay focused.
- Be flexible, adjust quickly, and capitalize on new prospecting activities.

Activities

Schedule weekly and daily activities related to:

- Finding targeted prospects.
- Getting introductions and referrals to targeted prospects.
- Getting face-to-face with targeted prospects.
- Networking.

Skills

Primarily through doing, learn the key skills related to high-impact prospecting methods:

- Networking.
- Asking for and getting introductions.
- Asking for and getting referrals.
- Handling the first face-to-face meeting.
- Proving your competence to a targeted prospect.
- Closing the sale.
- Refining your image.

You may be saying, "This all seems simple enough," and you're right: It *is* simple. There's nothing complicated about becoming a Rainmaker—*provided* you overcome any emotional, attitudinal and behavioral impediments. Unfortunately, these impediments frequently form the foundation of various avoidance tactics.

Top 5 Avoidance Tactics

1. **"I am not a Huckster."** In the legal and financial services realm, many people deny or denigrate the importance of actively recruiting new clients—*of selling*. "Salesman" is a dirty word, and selling is tantamount to prostitution. Well, this ain't necessarily so. Regardless of the title printed on your business card— financial consultant, wealth manager, partner or vice president—selling is *not* beneath you. It's a key component of your job. And if your salesmanship is seamless, you'll never be tarred with the same brush as a used-car salesman or the characters from "Glengarry Glen Ross."

    Sam was a proud man who thought selling smacked of desperation. A military school graduate and 17-year veteran, Sam had launched a second career as a financial planner when he approached me for coaching. I prescribed a regimen of high-impact activities, including face-to-face meetings with key clients to obtain introductions and referrals. But Sam kept dropping the ball when it came time for action. Whenever I wanted to review what he'd done the previous week, he talked in circles or insisted that I "teach something new today."

    I called him on it. "You've gotten away with talking in circles to a lot of people, haven't you?" Dead silence. "You're talking in circles to me, and you're not going to get away with it. I'm asking if you've performed A, B and C, and you're not answering my question. If you're not doing A, B and C, there's no way in the world you're going to become a Rainmaker." Then there was a long pause. "Yeah, you're right. You know, you're the first person who's called me on that," etc.

So we set the activities again, but he never fulfilled his commitments. Like an old soldier, he slowly faded away—his mother was sick, he didn't have time for a conference call, then *he* was sick. It reached the point where his assistant was embarrassed for him, but Sam just wouldn't do what was required. Why not? Further probing uncovered the real reason. He was afraid of looking like a salesman, afraid of asking somebody for business at his church, afraid of even developing a relationship that could lead to a sale. He was like the high-school kid who doesn't want to seem desperate for a date, and spends his Saturday nights at home alone.

During the "Dot.com Bull Market" of the late 1990s, it was easy for individuals—and entire companies—to deny that selling was important. There was little danger in the denial. After all, many firms had affluent prospects lining up outside their offices, pockets brimming with cash. During that bull market, anyone and everyone was making so much money that selling was nearly effortless—the wind was at their backs, full time.

In the wake of September 11 and the Dot.com Crash, the wind is in our faces, and it is past time to refine our selling skills. But in order to refine our selling skills, we must make peace with ourselves about the concept of selling. Greg is still wrestling with this issue, and as a result, he's still struggling to become a Rainmaker. Selling done properly is one of the oldest and most honorable professions. Just because "mamma" didn't raise you to be a salesperson, doesn't mean you can't change her mind by out-earning your doctor neighbor.

Everyone must raise his or her game, because everyone is targeting the affluent and the emerging affluent. That's where the money is. But to win affluent business, you must get them to like you, trust you, and respect you as a professional in today's environment. (I know I've already said that, and I promise to say it again.)

2. **Low-Impact "Busywork."** Social self-consciousness often leads people to use low-impact activities that keep the affluent at arm's length. Social self-consciousness involves feelings of intimidation in the presence of people of wealth, power and influence. Most of those who suffer from social self-consciousness have developed an inferiority complex. At some level, they've decided that affluent people are their economic and social "betters." As a result, they feel uncomfortable associating with wealthy prospects, much less trying to sell to them. In the financial services arena, social self-consciousness is fairly common—probably because so many professionals come from blue-collar backgrounds.

Terry personifies social self-consciousness. He wears expensive suits and drives a luxury car. And, although his first wife was a physician, he never did any business with his wife's centers-of-influence or the medical profession, because he didn't like doctors. "I always felt like they were talking down to me, looking down their noses at me. We didn't have anything in common." That was his rationale. Later, he married an attractive young waitress from a trendy restaurant, who was impressed with his status and income—relative to hers.

When I started work with Terry, I helped him profile the type of client he wanted to target, and suggested he join a country club in his area. But he wouldn't join a country club, because it was "too snooty." Instead, against my advice, he purchased a high-net-worth mailing list. I'm not opposed to such mailing lists, as long as you recognize their limitations. In my view, the only reason to purchase such a list is to gather data on "known quantities"—your acquaintances, friends of your friends, or friends of your clients. You should *not* use them for cold calls or unsolicited direct-mail campaigns. Terry would hear none of this. He simply sent out the mailings, and reaped his reward—nada.

Once recognized, social self-consciousness is relatively easy to overcome. Begin by eliminating all those "I don't like doctors" comments you use to avoid stepping into the world of the affluent. Then look for opportunities to rub shoulders with the wealthy, and take advantage of every opportunity you find. As you spend time in their world, your social self-consciousness will diminish.

3. **Focusing on the Sizzle, Not the Steak.** Some salespeople defer to the supposed selling power of PowerPoint presentations, brochures, websites and other collateral materials. They rely on their marketing departments, they hire consultants to teach them to write 78-word elevator speeches and value propositions—propositions so vague that I call them The Financial Lord's Prayer—"We deliver peace, prosperity and peace of mind for our clients, etc., etc." These statements contain everything but specifics and clear language.

   More often than not, you end up with a slick brochure boasting about all these wealth-management financial processes and products—many of which you don't really offer, and few of which you can speak intelligently about—so you're entire presentation comes off as nothing but sizzle without the steak. Worse, you look like someone who doesn't know what he's talking about—someone who's not nearly up to speed. Your prospect sits there, thinking "Huh? What's this guy talking about?" Then he mentally tattoos a big "S" onto your forehead—which stands for "sucker" and/or "salesperson."

   If you're one of those people who resists being "sold," you're not alone. The affluent also hate salespeople. That's why the true Rainmaker is so refined, and his presentation so well honed, that the entire process is perfectly seamless.

4. **Paralyzed by Preparation.** "If I could just read one more book, attend one more class, create another new brochure, fine-tune my PowerPoint presentation, *then* I'd be really prepared to prospect." Not really, because people afflicted with preparation paralysis always think they need to learn more, work on the per-

fect presentation, or wait for the perfect brochure. This is another avoidance behavior that grows out of fear. Like General McClellan, these folks are forever drilling for the big battle—the one they never plan to fight. And even if they did fight, it's a good bet their well-laid plans would fall apart on first contact with the prospect. The Rainmaker does his homework and gathers "intel," but she's also flexible enough to respond to unexpected questions and situations. Rainmakers learn best in the midst of the action.

5. **It's *Never* the Right Moment.** This guy can never find an appropriate "opening" that lets him steer the conversation toward business. Nor, for that matter, can he ever find the appropriate time or place. Bill was typical.

Bill was taking Tae Kwon Do classes as a prospecting activity, where he engaged the wealthy owner of a woodworking company in a 20-minute conversation. He listened carefully as the man talked about his personal and business life. But that's where it ended. When his partner asked why he hadn't talked about business, Bill exploded: "You can't just talk about goddamn business!"

When Bill recounted the story to me, I responded, "You did a good job of gathering 'intel' on this guy, but you need to improve your game. You should have said, "Hey, my partner's into woodworking [which he was]. Would it be possible for us to drop by your shop one of these days for a short tour? I know my partner would love that." Bill was delighted. "I can do that tomorrow night when I see him."

"Bingo!" I said. "Now you have your Rainmaker antenna out." Without intervention, Bill might have romanced this prospect forever, thinking there was never a real opportunity to talk business.

I'm not suggesting you hand out business cards to everyone who says hello in the supermarket. But once you've targeted your ideal prospect, it's important to arrange face-to-face activities with strategic intent. By strategic intent, I mean zeroing in on somebody you'd like as a client. Maybe this person attends the same health club, and you know each other well enough to say "hi." If so, your mission is to figure out a way to engage in conversation with the person, and get to know the person better, with the *strategic intent* of eventually sitting down to talk business—to put that individual into your pipeline at some point.

Fear of rejection, fear of failure, fear of getting outside your comfort zone, of playing without a net—these are powerful disincentives to developing the Rainmaker mindset, and they manifest themselves through avoidance behavior.

Remember, Rainmakers are made, not born. Their self-awareness fuels their understanding that fear can only be conquered by playing through it, and refusing to be held back. They may not be comfortable in every situation. They may be socially self-conscious. But they remain focused on their goals. They make mistakes, and they sometimes blow big opportunities, but they stay energized for tomorrow.

Most of all, they keep their antennae out at all times.

RAM: Rainmaker Avoidance Mindset Profile

This brief assessment focuses on situations, thoughts and actions that shape the Rainmaker Mindset. The exercise will help you determine whether you tend to play it safe within your comfort zone, or whether you're developing the mindset of a warrior—a fearless Rainmaker who plays without a net.

RAM Instructions: Don't simply answer as you think you should. To truly benefit from this exercise, it's important to answer each statement honestly.

For each statement, do you . . .

4—Strongly Agree

3—Agree

2—Disagree

1—Strongly Disagree

When you have completed all 12 statements, add up the circled numbers.

	4	3	2	1
1. I have hired, or would like to hire, a junior associate to be responsible for marketing.	4	3	2	1
2. I don't like the idea that anyone might perceive me as a salesperson.	4	3	2	1
3. It is very important that I hold industry designations (CFP, CLU, etc.).	4	3	2	1
4. I find it difficult to delegate.	4	3	2	1
5. Too much of my time is spent servicing non-affluent clients.	4	3	2	1
6. Lines of responsibility within my team are not as clear as they could be.	4	3	2	1
7. We have spent a lot of time, energy, and money on our brochure, at the expense of prospecting.	4	3	2	1
8. We need to be more congruent with our value proposition.	4	3	2	1
9. We spend hours on our business plan, but don't always execute based on it.	4	3	2	1
10. We always strive to create the "perfect" presentation materials (pitch book).	4	3	2	1
11. The situation must be right in order for me to feel comfortable talking business.	4	3	2	1
12. In social situations I often let business opportunities pass.	4	3	2	1

Add up the circled numbers and enter the total here. RAM Score = _____

Look for the range below into which your RAM Score fits. The description is an indication of how the above situations, thoughts and actions are impacting your progress toward becoming a Rainmaker.

RAM Score	Action Plan
40—48	You are in a high state of Rainmaker avoidance. Your thoughts and actions are holding you back in many ways. Read and re-read Section II on the Mindset of a Rainmaker, and commit to making one positive change at a time.
32—39	You are in a moderate state of Rainmaker avoidance, which has you putting off important Rainmaker activities. Select two to three of the areas where your score is highest, and commit to action that will significantly improve that area.
23—31	You are halfway between a Rainmaker's mindset and avoidance. As a Rainmaker wannabe, you can move forward with a little effort. Focus on doing the activities you tend to put off, and you will quickly enable your Rainmaker mindset to take charge.
16—22	You are doing a good job of staying focused on your Rainmaking tasks. Concentrate on fine-tuning one or two of the areas with higher scores. Select areas where you can improve.
12—15	The Sky's The Limit! You're doing well. Keep raising the bar.

SUMMARY

Financial advisors who are reluctant to prospect are much more likely to describe high-impact activities as *extremely challenging*, whereas few of those eager to prospect agree with that statement. What's more, financial advisors reluctant to use high-impact methods were also less likely to acquire new affluent clients.

There's nothing complicated about becoming a Rainmaker—*provided* you overcome any emotional, attitudinal and behavioral impediments.

My Top 5 Avoidance Tactics include: (1) Denying or denigrating the importance of sales activities; (2) Distracting yourself with low-impact busywork to avoid face-to-face encounters; (3) Focusing on the sizzle, not the steak; (4) Becoming paralyzed with preparation; and (5) Failing to make or seize opportunities to talk business. Be honest with yourself, and recognize avoidance tactics for what they are.

Research Facts

▶ 50% of financial advisors who are reluctant to prospect said finding prospects was "extremely challenging"; only 11% of those eager to prospect felt the same way.

▶ Obtaining introductions and referrals, and getting face-to-face with prospects was "extremely challenging" for just 1% of those eager to prospect. Those numbers are 26% and 52% respectively, for reluctant prospectors.

▶ Handling face-to-face meetings, proving competency to prospects and closing sales were deemed challenging by zero percent of eager prospectors.

TAKING ACTION

- Recognize any avoidance tactics you use, and commit to implementing the Rainmaker Game Plan.
- Take the Assessment above to learn if you make any of the most common mindset mistakes. Be honest with yourself.
- Unless you scored "Sky's the limit!" on the Rainmaker Avoidance Mindset assessment, commit to a specific action plan in order to eliminate any avoidance tendencies.

4

Developing the Mindset of a Warrior

Rick had just graduated from Duke University with a degree in accounting. His first thought was to pass the requirements for becoming a certified public accountant. After successfully passing his CPA exam, Rick went on his first and only job interview with one of the prestigious "Big 4" accounting firms. The interview lasted only five minutes, but it changed Rick's life.

Rick was hired conditionally for one year. The requirements were quite simple. He was handed a folder that contained a list of businesses and told he had 12 months to bring in 15 of these companies as new clients. "By the time I reached the parking lot, the thrill of being hired was gone. I felt as though I had a gun to my head," recalled Rick. He was a highly educated CPA, and he was ready for any challenge related to his professional expertise. Instead, Rick was being pushed outside his CPA comfort zone and forced to sell.

Rick would not allow himself to quit his first job. For one thing, his mother would have killed him. Secondly, he wanted to stick it in his manager's face at year-end. When Rick expressed that to me, I knew he had just taken the first crucial step into the Mindset of a Rainmaker.

Rick had activated his *achievement cycle* by having a "big hairy audacious goal" thrust upon him and then, rather than crumbling under the weight, determining that he would do whatever was necessary to achieve the goal. This meant he was forced to act *way* outside of his comfort zone and engage in activities with which he was completely unfamiliar and unsure. Rick quickly realized that his first course of action was to get in front of the decision makers of these companies. From there, he would have to learn how to sell them on his firm.

With no other tools than the brains of a Duke graduate, and fueled by abject fear of failure, Rick was able to immediately engage in prospecting activities. His goal focus enabled him to stay the course, even when he wasn't sure what to do. Failure was not an option. It's what kept him going when his thinking was negative and his confidence was non-existent. It's what propelled him into action when he didn't feel like it.

Rick never allowed himself to get tangled in *preparation paralysis.* Instead, he eagerly tapped the power of learning through doing. By admitting the fear, remaining focused on his goal (even though it was imposed upon him), and doing what he considered necessary for success, he was developing the mindset of a Rainmaker. He was activating the Rainmaker's Achievement Cycle without even realizing it. This is a cycle that anyone can master—anyone with the sincere desire to become a Rainmaker, that is.

Within a year, Rick emerged as a true Rainmaker. He brought in 12 new clients, not 15, but surpassed everyone's expectations, and his CPA firm was delighted. Rick was hired on a permanent basis—not as a CPA, but as a Rainmaker.

By his early forties, Rick had retired. He had acquired such a level of personal affluence for himself and his family that he decided to devote the rest of his life to his two passions: family and golf.

The Rainmaker's Achievement Cycle

After years of observing the prospecting habits of the financial professionals he'd managed, Albert E. N. Gray told his 1940 NALU Convention audience, "The common denominator of success—the secret of success of every man who has ever been successful—lies in the fact that he formed the habit of doing things that failures don't like to do." I'm sure that Albert Gray's comments would have been gender inclusive today, but the wisdom of his words is timeless.

Achieving our goals is determined by the interaction of three components: how we feel, what we think, and what we do. The reason the Rainmaker Mindset is so critical is that most people tend to act on how they feel at the moment. If the activities associated with Rainmaking are new, unfamiliar and challenging, it's difficult to feel positive and confident about them. When negative feelings emerge from our subconscious, they focus us on all the excuses that justify remaining in our comfort zone. This usually causes us to immerse ourselves—time after time—in comfortable activities in order to reduce our anxieties. This is a Non-Rainmaker's Achievement Cycle, and you're about to break free from this pattern of feeling → thinking → doing. Activating your Rainmaker's Achievement Cycle looks like this.

Activating your Rainmaker's Achievement Cycle reverses the non-achievement process because it changes the sequence from:

feeling → thinking → doing

to

doing → thinking → feeling

You accomplish this profound "mind shift" by linking everything you do to a strong goal focus. That's how you break out of your comfort zone—by performing Rainmaker activities linked to your goal of acquiring 10+ affluent clients over the next 12 months. Regardless of how you feel or what you're thinking at any given moment, keep that goal in front of you, and do what you know is necessary. Once you've fixed your goals and the right activities, "Yours is not to question why, yours is but to do—or die." In other words, you can only "die" by succumbing to anxiety and failing to "do."

Performing high-impact activities when you don't want to, when you don't feel comfortable, when your will is as sluggish as Mississippi Mud Pie, is key to developing a Rainmaker's mindset, and therefore, a Rainmaker's success. Anyone can engage in high-impact activities when he or she "feels" like it—much the same as anyone can exercise when he or she "feels" like it. Rainmakers do what is necessary *when it's necessary*, even if they'd rather be doing almost anything else.

Let's activate your Rainmaker's Achievement Cycle. The first and most critical step is setting a goal—a BIG goal that you commit to with your heart and soul. Failure cannot be an option. Since acquiring 10+ new affluent clients over 12 months is my definition of a Rainmaker, be like Rick and commit to bringing in 15 new affluent clients. That would be your target if you were attending our Rainmaker Institute.

This target (your Rainmaker goal) should make you feel extremely uncomfortable. It's typical for a new Rainmaker to experience a surge of adrenaline coupled with a knot in her stomach. Think of it as good discomfort, since it means you are serious about achieving your Rainmaking goals. Minimal or no discomfort usually translates into lack of genuine commitment.

Subsequent chapters will enable you to determine what activities you need to be doing, and the skills you need to develop. At this juncture, it's only important that you fully sense the true power of the "achievement cycle," and how instinctive it is in every one of us. We all have the capacity to re-engage this cycle. Therefore, everyone has the ability to become a Rainmaker. I say "re-engage," because this cycle is not exclusive to Rainmakers. It's used to achieve every major goal that every person has ever sought. The difference between high achievers and the "masses" is quite simple: high achievers continually re-engage their "achievement cycle."

Generic Patterns of Achievement

I want you to reflect on your past, and select two achievements that have given you a sense of pride. As you revisit these achievements, recall the anxiety and pressure placed on you from the sheer weight of these goals. Think of the activities you were forced to perform to accomplish these goals. Recall your thoughts, even that little devilish voice of doubt ("You can't do this") whispering in your ear. Remember how you felt (feelings) as you broke through your comfort zone to do whatever was necessary.

What you will probably discover is that you've just embarked on a pleasant journey down memory lane. To help replicate this same process—a process you've already used successfully at some point in your life—complete the chart entitled "My Past Achievements" below. Here are the instructions:

- Achievements #1 and #2—Describe your achievement (goal accomplishment) and the time frame from beginning to completion.
- Activities—List the specific tasks and ongoing activities you had to perform in order to complete each achievement.
- Pattern of Use—State how often you undertook each task and activity. Was it daily, weekly, monthly or yearly?
- Skills Required & Developed—Describe the competencies you needed to realize each achievement. What skills did you have to learn? Recall how you learned each skill.

My Past Achievements

Achievement #1: _____

Activities   Pattern of Use

_____

_____

_____

_____

Skills Required & Developed:

_____

_____

_____

_____

Achievement #2: _____

Activities   Pattern of Use

_____

_____

_____

_____

Skills Required & Developed:

_____

_____

_____

_____

What this exercise demonstrates is the power of doing specific activities linked to your goal. It emphasizes that once a goal becomes imprinted in the mind, it morphs into a positive obsession. Regardless whether the goal is self-imposed or thrust upon you (as Rick's was), the process is the same. The goal forces you to do activities before you have proof that you can succeed. This is a key component of the Rainmaker's mindset: believing without proof—taking a genuine leap of faith.

Another feature of the "Achievement Cycle" is how it activates our endorphins to stimulate every aspect of our being. Whenever we actively engage in the pursuit of a major goal, we come alive, we get energized, no matter how hard we work or how far outside the comfort zone we're forced to venture. I know you've experienced this in the past two achievements you just revisited. Now you're going to activate this psychic energy as a Rainmaker.

SUMMARY

Everyone is capable of developing the mindset of a Rainmaker! You've already achieved past goals that required a similar state of mind, a commitment with your heart and soul. As you recalled past achievements, you've just reconnected with nature's gift to mankind, the "Achievement Cycle."

It's time, therefore, to re-activate this achievement cycle as it relates to your Rainmaking goals. If you're not feeling queasy, you either aren't thinking big enough, or you're not fully committed. Nobody has ever developed the mindset of a Rainmaker with a casual commitment.

Rick became a Rainmaker because it was thrust upon him. "I felt like I had a gun to my head," was how he described the first year of learning his craft. Let Rick serve as an inspiration to you and anyone else looking to master his/her craft. You must be willing to do whatever is required—even when you don't want to, when your thinking isn't as positive as you would like, or your faith is floundering. This is what separates true Rainmakers from wannabes.

Research Facts

Of the ANAC respondents who were reluctant to prospect:

▶ 60% added zero clients with investable assets of $1 million or more.

▶ 50% were extremely challenged in finding affluent prospects.

▶ 52% were extremely challenged in obtaining face-to-face meetings with affluent prospects.

TAKING ACTION

Your first step in developing the mindset of a Rainmaker is to establish your client acquisition goal for the upcoming year. If you're struggling with this step, the following three-step process will help.

Step 1: Client Acquisition Profile. Describe in as much detail as possible the profile of the new affluent client you want to target: investable assets, age, occupation, specific needs, unique niche, etc.

Step 2: Client Acquisition Goal. Determine the number of new clients that you want to acquire during the next 12 months who fit this profile. Hint: think of Rick and his goal of 15.

Step 3: Personal Reward. Calculate the monetary benefit from achieving the goal of Step 2, and determine what kind of reward you'll give yourself for accomplishing that goal.

The Activities of a Rainmaker

5

Common Sense,
But Not Common Practice

*The affluent reported serious gaps between their expectations
and the performance of their primary financial advisors.*

—Factoid, 2004 APD Research

As a veteran financial advisor, Larry enjoyed a healthy income, belonged to two country clubs, and drove a brand new 7-Series BMW. To project exactly the right image, Larry worked with an advertising agency to create what he now calls "a beautiful $15,000 puff piece that has cost me business."

Larry was right: his new brochure was beautiful. It described how he could provide every conceivable wealth management service, creating the expectation that he offered something very special. He couldn't wait to begin using it. However, the results were not what he anticipated. Within two weeks, Larry lost an existing client and an affluent prospect who had come to him through a referral.

Larry met with his client, presented his new brochure, and began talking about all the new services he was going to provide. His client, who was a business owner, peppered him with probing questions that Larry found difficult to answer. The client ended the meeting by saying that he was not confident in Larry's ability to deliver all those services, and was going to close his account. Larry's referred prospect also asked detailed questions prompted by the brochure. Once again, Larry stumbled, and that's all it took.

Larry learned the hard way that affluent investors look beyond image, and focus on substance. *You must be as advertised!*

The Real Deal

Most financial firms and other service professionals know what they must do to consistently attract, service and retain affluent clients. They spend millions saying so in their advertising. But advertising raises expectations, and our APD survey respondents have sent a clear message about that: To secure our long-term business, *you must walk the talk* by becoming fully competent in providing solutions. You must deliver value by offering the necessary range of services.

Larry's client terminated his account for two important reasons. First of all, by Larry's admission to me, the client had not been receiving the best of service. Larry tried to use his new brochure to assure his client that things would now be different, but it took only a few pointed questions for his client to determine otherwise. Needless to say, Larry not only lost income, but a valuable source of introductions and referrals.

Some service providers aren't prepared to serve the affluent, because they haven't raised their games. Terry, our doctor-phobic wealth manager from Chapter 3, was another such person. Terry wasn't comfortable with his deliverables, because he hadn't taken time to upgrade his services. He wanted to pursue affluent clients, but in reality, he was basically a stockbroker pretending to be a wealth manager. In addition, he was a little too enamored with the path of least resistance—chasing the short-term buck. He's the kind of guy who will promise anything to secure the business, and then ignore your account—until the next time he needs a fee or commission.

When deciding whether to use the same service provider again, our APD respondents gave the strongest influence to:

- Any problems I encountered were resolved quickly and satisfactorily.
- They provided good service following my purchase.
- They previously provided information I needed to make a satisfactory decision.

Of all the findings from the APD Research, the most surprising was our respondents' intense skepticism toward basic sales and marketing techniques—especially when it comes to intangibles (services). Another surprising result was their level of consumer savvy. You might think people with high disposable incomes would conduct less research—and would be less discerning—since they can "afford" to make mistakes. The opposite is true. The affluent are *more* discerning, because they've really learned from past mistakes. But as crusty and defensive as these wealthy prospects can be, *they will do almost anything for you once you prove yourself*—once you break down the barriers and develop a relationship based on mutual trust and professional respect.

Bottom line: Don't even think of prospecting face-to-face until you can deliver on your promises.

The Prospecting Hierarchy

Hang up the phone, and stop the presses. Low-impact prospecting activities deserve low priority.

As Chart 4 illustrates, ANAC respondents achieved substantially better results using high-impact activities. Targeted networking, referrals and introductions brought in twice—even three times—the number of clients as direct mail and cold calling. Once again, all evidence points to the importance of developing close relationships with affluent clients and prospects.

Chart 4		
Prospecting Methods: Use and Results		
Prospecting Method	**Percentage who USED this Method**	**Percentage who Brought in NEW CLIENTS using this Method**
Direct Mail	57%	27%
Cold Calling	46%	27%
Seminars	62%	40%
Networking*	93%	78%
Asking for Referrals*	97%	90%
Asking for Introductions*	91%	72%
*High-Impact Activities		

Targeted Networking

Before launching your networking efforts, it's important to create a profile of the type of client you want. Examine your top 25 clients (see exercise on pages 61-62), and develop profiles based on key demographic factors—income levels, investable assets, etc. Then search for ways and means of adding more clients like those. Ideally, you will tap existing clients—your affluent "centers-of-influence"—for introductions and referrals.

In addition, I recommend consulting the Cap Gemini report to develop lists of high-net-worth prospects in your area.

Wealth Categories
Cap Gemini Ernst & Young 2002

Category	Available Investable Assets
HNW 1	$10 million and higher
HNW 2	$1 to $10 million
Mass Affluent	$500 thousand to $1 million
Emerging Affluent 1	$250 thousand to $500 thousand
Emerging Affluent 2	$100 thousand to $250 thousand
Upper Middle Class	$75 thousand to $100 thousand
Middle Class	$25 thousand to $75 thousand
Lower Middle Class	Under $25 thousand

*

Not only should you use the Cap Gemini report for your prospecting, you will find it a valuable guide in developing your Ideal Client Profile following the guidelines outlined below. This will also help guide your thinking when examining your top 25 clients.

Develop an Ideal Client Profile

Create a potential profit analysis by identifying those clients who:

(1) Produced the highest levels of gross commissions or fees during the past 12 months.

(2) Have the highest levels of total assets on your books.

(3) Have the potential for more gross commissions, fees and/or assets in the next 12 months that would be comparable to, or higher than, the above.

This will help you see where potential might lie, and determine your cut-off points.

Next, determine where time and resources are being allocated. Where is your time going? Is it to add value to clients that qualify according to your potential profit analysis? Conduct this two-week exercise at the same time you perform your profit analysis.

(1) Log every incoming call.
(2) Time the length of each call.
(3) Log the nature of the call.
(4) Determine the time to fulfill what, if anything, was requested.

During the third week, hold a team meeting to review your findings. By this time, you should know the revenue/asset characteristics of your desired client base, giving you an idea of whom you want to deal with. These are the clients who will appreciate your value, allow you to get paid, and respect your time and professionalism. Odds are that you'll be shocked by your findings. One financial advisor discovered that he was devoting 90% of his time to non-profitable clients!

As I stated earlier, purchasing a high-income mailing list isn't a *terrible* idea—in and of itself—so long as you use the list to target affluent business and social acquaintances, friends of friends, etc. for your future high-impact activities.

After conducting careful reconnaissance, the Rainmaker learns the names of the "power players" in her community. She knows where they live and where they play, as well as the associations, civic organizations and charities to which they devote their time and money. In other words, the Rainmaker really does her homework before joining the Lions, Rotary Club, Chamber of Commerce or merchants association. She goes where the affluent prospects are. She doesn't join just any organization: she joins the right ones.

A common mistake among Rainmaker wannabes is joining a dozen different groups willy-nilly in an effort to "cover all the bases." That's hardly targeted networking. Once you join an organization, high-impact prospecting demands that you really get involved with the group's activities. If you become a member of the most powerful Rotary Club in town, your first task is to ask someone in the know:

- The main functions that the organization supports.
- Which major committee(s) to join.
- The names of the committee(s) leaders.

- The kind of work/skills/commitment needed by the committee(s).

Your next assignment is to become *very involved* in that committee's work—to become a worker bee. That's why you should network within just a handful of "the best" organizations. You won't have time for more.

Wait about six months (my rule of thumb) before you even *begin* talking business with other members. If they talk business with you, that's fine. But you won't initiate such discussions until six months have passed. All too often, people arrive at their first meeting, and start dispensing business cards like a gumball machine.

Remember, your task is to build relationships—to create emotional equity with the movers and shakers. If you've chosen the right organizations, you'll have plenty of opportunities to casually communicate what you do with the people you've targeted. Most people go wrong because they join low-grade networking groups packed with salespeople, who waste time referring themselves to one another. These groups are like the parties organized by the nerdy fraternities—the event is advertised as a great way to meet girls, but the only people who show up are geeky guys.

FYI: there's no rule that says you can't form your own networking organization. One of my clients launched a fly fishing club after he discovered that several clients shared his interest in the hobby. The club has been a marvelous networking tool: existing members often bring new prospects to meetings and on fishing trips across the country.

Chart 5		
Hierarchy of Affluent Prospecting Methods		
LOW Impact	**MODERATE Impact**	**HIGH Impact**
• Direct Mail • Cold Calling	• Targeted Seminars	• Networking • Referrals • Introductions

Introductions and Referrals

A Rainmaker is part detective, all relationship, and very well-rehearsed. His approach to selling is so seamless that you can't detect any gaps—you can't pinpoint where the sales pitch leaps out.

There's an important distinction between referrals and introductions. Asking for referrals is more basic, needs less preparation, takes less courage, and requires less commitment from the service provider and the client. An introduction is by far the most effective high-impact method for acquiring new million-dollar relationships.

In Chapter 8, I'll walk you through a skill session that will help you develop the finesse you need to get affluent introductions and referrals—the kind of finesse that Rainmaker wannabes don't have. But before I involve you with skill training, you have some Rainmaking activity work to complete.

Since two of the most important high-impact activities are introductions and referrals, and since most of these come from your top clients, I've found that the best way to start is by taking an inventory of your top 25 clients. Let's face it, what Rainmakers continually strive to do is replicate their top 25 clients. The form below is identical to the one I use in our Rainmaker Institute. Take your time. Make certain you are thoughtful *and* accurate as you work through this exercise. Much of your future Rainmaking success will be a direct result of this effort.

Top 25 Client Inventory

Name: _____

Number of Affluent Clients acquired from this client's Introductions/Referrals: ____

How this client benefits from your services: _____

This client's Centers-of-Influence: _____

Potential for receiving additional Introductions/Referrals from this client: _____

Now that you know which of your top clients has actually been responsible for new affluent relationships coming your way, you will want to use the "Rainmaker's Rule of Six," which states that each of your top 25 clients should be responsible for providing six new clients during the lifespan of your professional relationship. This is your rule of thumb for getting introductions and referrals. Granted, some clients will have their fingerprints on a dozen or more, while others will fall short of six. But it's important to imprint the Rainmaker's Rule of Six on your mind, since this creates a strong belief and a strong expectation.

Once you imprint this rule on your mind, you're now fully armed and dangerous. Now, it's time to learn about the Top 25 Introduction Notebook.

Top 25 Introduction Notebook

This tool will enable you to immediately execute the "Rainmaker Rule of Six," and with a high degree of effectiveness. All you need is a spiral notebook, the kind your kids use in school, to create a detailed profile of each of your top 25 clients. Your first step is to label this notebook: *Top 25 Introduction Book*. Dedicate one page per client to allow room for all that client's family details. You can keep this simple, like the sample page below:

Matt Oechsli—consultant-author-speaker—sports fan
Sandy Oechsli—spouse—bookkeeper—knitter—cat & bird lover
Heidi Oechsli—daughter, 23 years old—MBA student @ UNC-Greensboro
Amy Oechsli—daughter, 20 years old—junior @ NC State—Raleigh
Patrick Oechsli—son, 15 years old—sophomore in HS, baseball player

- Barry Finch—golfing buddy—12/1/05
  —owns an auto parts store
- Larry Smalley—golfing buddy—12/1/05
  —cardiologist

The drill is simple: in a conversation with your client (Matt Oechsli), you were able to uncover the names and some basic background on two of his golfing partners. Rather than trust your memory, you recorded this prospecting information on Matt's page in your *Top 25 Introduction Book*. You will want to include as much information about Barry and Larry as your intelligence gathering provides. Always remember to include the date as a point of reference, both for you and your client.

After documenting this background information, schedule a "to-do" activity on your calendar—for example, to call Matt two weeks from the entry date, and ask for an introduction to his golfing buddies. Obviously, you should exercise some skill when doing so (I've included a sample script in Chapter 7), but it doesn't have to be more complicated than some small talk followed by, "I'd like to meet your golfing partners, Barry and Larry. Let's play a round at my course—my treat."

Earlier, I stated that the *Top 25 Introduction Notebook* was highly effective. I lied. It's 100% effective! That's right: every rainmaking student who has applied this high-impact activity has discovered that he always gets the high-impact face-to-face introduction. Rainmakers refine the skills required for this activity by *doing*. This doesn't mean they are 100% successful at getting the business. But Rainmakers are fully aware that they are operating at a high level, selling is still a numbers game. However, consistently performing these high-impact activities leads to 10 or more new ideal clients a year.

Take Time for the "Extra-Curricular"

"Golf, baseball games, charitable foundations and civic organizations? Who has time for all that? I've got a business to run, and existing accounts to manage—not to mention a spouse and children."

It's true. High-impact prospecting can make big demands on your time. That's why it's important to exploit *targeted* activities and opportunities. Obviously, you can't spend each workday eating hotdogs at the ballpark with every Tom, Dick and Sally. On the other hand, keep your Rainmaker antennae tuned for major opportunities—especially when they're disguised as recreation. This isn't always easy. Peter still has trouble dragging himself out of the office.

He was recently invited on a week-long ski trip to Aspen, Colorado by a wealthy "center-of-influence" client—someone who could deliver introductions and referrals. Despite the lessons learned at the wedding, Peter was reluctant to spend so much time out of the office. When Peter hesitated, his client said, "Are you f—king nuts? You can't *not* go! You're going to be with eight other people that ALL qualify as affluent. You'll want to get to know them, to be in their centers-of-influence, to become buddies with them. You're going to get business from them."

Still, Peter was hesitant, and decided to call me. I said to him, "You're just hesitating because you haven't done this kind of high-level rainmaking before. Intellectually, you know you should go, but emotionally you're thinking, "I can't get out of the office, I'm trying to run my business." I told him to go, and—surprise, surprise—he picked up substantial new business.

What would have happened if Greg had received this invitation? Would he have gone on the trip? Probably not. If he did go, would he perform the right rainmaking activities—developing relationships with people and putting them into his pipeline? Probably not. He would have gone skiing—period.

Actually, even if Greg had stumbled onto a client like Peter's, he probably wouldn't have known how to use that client. Many professionals have one or two clients like this, and don't even realize it. Fewer still take advantage of these relationships. What a waste!

Consider Peter's client. He and Peter had become good friends, because the client liked him as a person, trusted him as a person, and really respected his professionalism. When you have those three components, a good client will do anything for you. And this one went the extra mile, becoming an advocate and a prospector for Peter—practically forcing him along on that ski trip.

True Rainmakers continually expand their centers-of-influence to bring in new business. Thanks to their close relationships with powerful clients, they need only ask, "Hey Phil, who do I need to know?" And the best clients will supply a regular stream of personal introductions and referrals.

RAP: Rainmaker Activity Profile

This brief assessment focuses on specific activities tied to Rainmaker success. The exercise will allow you to determine whether you're doing what you need to do, or letting less important activities distract you.

RAP Instructions: Don't answer as you think you should. Be totally honest about each response. For each statement, do you . . .

> 4—Strongly Agree
>
> 3—Agree
>
> 2—Disagree
>
> 1—Strongly Disagree

	4	3	2	1
1. I have analyzed my client base and identified my introduction and referral opportunities.	4	3	2	1
2. I am spending at least 70% of my time face-to-face with affluent clients, centers-of-influence, or qualified affluent prospects.	4	3	2	1
3. I engage in one "high-impact" Rainmaking activity every working day.	4	3	2	1
4. I always have my Rainmaker's antenna out, looking for new opportunities.	4	3	2	1
5. I restrict my prospecting activities only to high-impact activities.	4	3	2	1
6. I am constantly getting introduced to potential affluent clients.	4	3	2	1
7. I spend little or no time with smaller clients or prospects.	4	3	2	1

Add up the circled numbers and enter the total here. RAP Score = _____

Look for the range below in which your RAP Score fits. The description is an indication of how the above activities are impacting your progress toward becoming a Rainmaker.

RAP Score	Action Plan
25–28	Your Rainmaking activity is terrific. Keep up the good work, but always look to improve by fine-tuning one or two of the areas with lower scores.
21–24	You are above average in your Rainmaking activity. However, no Rainmaker can afford to be satisfied with an above-average activity level. Focus on doing the activities you tend to put off, and putting off less important activities that distract you.
16–20	Some activities you do; others you don't. That makes you average, and you don't want to accept that. Select two or three of the areas where your score is lowest and commit to incorporating those activities into your daily pattern. That will probably require getting rid of, or delegating, activities that are distracting you.
15 or below	There is no simple way to say it. Whatever you're doing, it's not what you need to be doing. Revisit Chapter 4, and reactivate your Rainmaker's Achievement Cycle. You need work on your goal commitment first, and then work on doing those "high-impact" activities.

SUMMARY

To attract and retain affluent clients, you must offer the depth and breadth of services that they desire. You must be as advertised—the real deal. Slick brochures and vague value propositions are no substitute for knowing your stuff, and communicating it directly and persuasively.

This means that you must come face-to-face with affluent prospects using high-impact activities—networking, introductions and referrals.

Taking inventory of your Top 25 clients is akin to preparing to dig for gold in your backyard—after determining that a vein of gold *does* run through your property. The Rainmaker's Rule of Six is a generalization that rainmakers take seriously. It provides both the awareness and focus required to effectively use your Top 25 Introduction Book. Make certain that every prospect name you enter into your introduction book is complete with a scheduled call-date between two and three weeks from the initial discovery of the person you want to meet.

Target your activities and opportunities, and apply subtle, seamless selling tactics using the skills you're going to fine-tune in the upcoming Skill Section. Once you develop close and personal relationships with major centers-of-influence, these clients will send a steady stream of new business your way.

Research Facts

▸ 97% of financial advisors brought in new clients through referrals. Only 27% obtain new clients via direct mail or cold calling.

▸ Only 40% of respondents landed new clients using seminars.

▸ When deciding whether to use the same service provider again, APD respondents gave the strongest influence to: (1) quick and satisfactory resolution of problems; and (2) providing good service following the original purchase.

TAKING ACTION

- Review your sales materials and website to determine if you really deliver the full range of services advertised. If you can't fulfill promises, don't make them. If you *can* deliver what you say, then be prepared to discuss your services in an intelligent manner, and answer any questions raised by skeptical prospects.
- Inventory your Top 25 clients and apply the Rainmaker's Rule of Six.
- Create a Top 25 Introduction Book.
- Talk to one Top 25 client a day, with a view toward getting face-to-face and uncovering a new name for your introduction book.
- Make a list of any "centers-of-influence" you already have. Schedule dates and times to engage in appropriate, non-threatening activities with them—activities that offer opportunities to solicit referrals and introductions.
- Target affluent prospects in your area, using the Cap Gemini report or mailing lists of high-net-worth individuals, and try to connect them to your Top 25 clients or your centers-of-influence.
- Research local professional, civic and charitable associations to determine if their members are worth targeting, and which of the organizations might be worth joining.
- Engage in one "high-impact" Rainmaking activity every day.

6

Maximize High-Impact Activities

As our research clearly shows, the prospecting methods that have the greatest impact are networking, asking for referrals, and asking for introductions. These were the methods used by the survey respondents who were able to produce significant Rainmaker results. Why? Because they are high-impact, direct-contact methods that enable you to go where the affluent are, connect with them, and orchestrate that first, all-important face-to-face meeting to "talk business."

We explored six prospecting methods in our research, but we know that other methods are being used—a total of 11 to be exact. The critical Rainmaker question is this: Are the prospecting methods you use enabling you to spend 70% of your time face-to-face with qualified affluent prospects, or with people who can refer you to qualified affluent prospects?

Now is the time to take inventory. Which of these 11 prospecting methods are you using? What results are you achieving?

Your best prospects are individuals who match your *Ideal Client Profile* and are experiencing, or about to experience, a business or life change that has significant financial implications. You want to meet affluent people who are in motion, who have something going on in their lives, or who are putting money in motion. The most effective way to connect with qualified affluent prospects at exactly the right moment is by focusing your prospecting activity on the five High-Impact Prospecting Methods. The focus of this chapter is on how to do that. It's important to remember how inextricably linked these high-impact activities are with the skills required to execute them.

Rainmaking Prospecting Impact

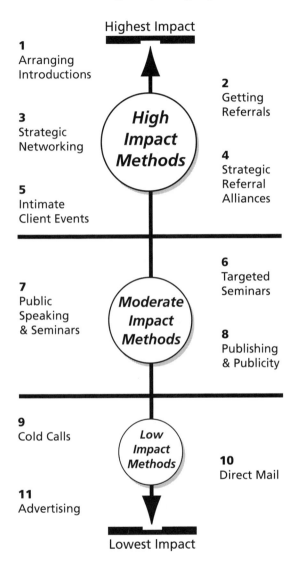

Arranging Introductions and Getting Referrals

Speed is not the only reason why introductions and referrals are at the top of your prospecting methods list. Another reason is *transfer of trust*. Studies show that when prospects are introduced or referred to you by someone they trust, they are more likely to grant you face-to-face meetings—and to disclose more information when you do meet.

Before you do anything else, make a list of:

- The clients from your Top 25 that you believe are a potential source of introductions and referrals.
- Other clients whose circle of influence might include affluent people who closely match your *Affluent Client Profile*.
- Family members, friends and acquaintances whose circles of influence might include affluent people who closely match your *Ideal Client Profile*.

With those lists "in hand," you essentially have **two strategies** for arranging introductions and getting referrals, and you should use both.

1. Ask for an Introduction or Referral.

   Go to people you know (clients and others) and ask them for introductions or referrals to people they know who closely match your *Ideal Client Profile*. To focus that effort, you can also identify specific business and life changes that would increase the likelihood that such people are ready to consider what you can do for them.

   When you **ask a client** for an introduction or referral, say something like . . .

   Matt, I'd like to meet your colleague Dan Vena. What's the best way for you to personally introduce me?

   Now, it's not an issue of whether they are willing; it's an issue of how to best arrange this introduction.

   If you must ask for a referral, select key business and/or life changes to which you could respond and demonstrate your competence quickly. Ask, "Who do you know that . . ." questions. For example, "Who do you know that . . .

   - *Is selling, or about to sell, a business?*
   - *Has recently switched jobs, and may need help with a 401(k) rollover?*

- *Is getting ready for retirement, and may need help with the transition?*
- *Is thinking about cashing in a stock option?*

And there is always . . .

- *Who do you know that is dissatisfied with their present financial advisors (attorneys, CPAs)?*

When you ask **family members, friends or acquaintances** who are not clients, they may have difficulty understanding exactly what you do and the value you bring to clients. Because you know these people well, don't hesitate to take the time to explain both.

- Use anecdotes, stories and case studies to communicate your value. Give them clear examples of how you solved client problems and helped them take advantage of opportunities to save money and grow their assets.

When a client, family member, friend or acquaintance provides you with a specific referral, always ask if he'd be willing to personally introduce you to that individual—and suggest the specific place and time for that introduction. That type of introduction requires the introducer's presence, so choose a time and location convenient for him, as well as for the targeted prospect. Simply say . . .

I'm really looking forward to talking with (prospect's name). Is there any way we could arrange a personal introduction—say, next Tuesday or Wednesday for lunch at a restaurant that's convenient for both of you?

2. Identify Affluent Individuals You Want to Meet.

This is where your *Top 25 Introduction Notebook* comes into play. As you identify specific affluent individuals who can be reached through the centers-of-influence of your clients, family members, friends and/or acquaintances, those individuals become entries in your notebook. Learn everything you can about those people, both professionally and personally. When investigating them, look also for the business and life changes that could create a financial impact point for you. Then ask the person who knows them to introduce you. If that isn't possible, ask for a referral.

Advisors often avoid asking for referrals and introductions because they assume their clients, family members, friends and acquaintances have a low threshold of referral tolerance. That is rarely the case! Everyone recognizes the importance of word-of-mouth in making purchase decisions. Most people are also aware that the National Do Not Call Registry makes it difficult to reach people by phone. Besides, when people like you and respect your professional competence, they'll be pleased that you asked, and eager to introduce or refer you to those they know.

Strategic Networking

Everyone networks. That's because we are naturally drawn to groups of people who share our interests and our concerns, and who include people we enjoy being with. Basically, those groups fall into three categories:

- *Social Groups*—Drawn together because of the activities, enjoyment and prestige the group provides.
- *Community Groups*—Drawn together in order to identify with, and contribute to, what the group represents.
- *Industry Groups*—Drawn together to participate in business-related activity, to learn and to pursue personal interests related to the technology and culture of that industry.

Strategic networking harnesses this natural pull, and gives it a different intent. By identifying the social, community and industry groups that contain people who match your *Ideal Client Profile* cluster, you can . . .

- Find ways to access and gain entry into those groups.
- Once inside, position yourself to attract attention, build friendships, use your expertise to serve their cause, and build trust.

As you become a known, respected and trusted member of the group, other members will actually seek out your services, and will gladly provide you with introductions and referrals to the people they know. Here's how it works.

Social Groups

The most effective entree into the social groups of the affluent is through a client, family member, friend or acquaintance who agrees to be an *internal advocate* for you. Your internal advocate takes you to the events and activities of the group, explains what's acceptable and unacceptable behavior, and introduces you to people who match your *Ideal Affluent Prospect Profile.* Most important, you need to know if asking people what kind of work they do, and responding with your 10-second introduction, is acceptable –and whether it's appropriate to exchange business cards. The more your internal advocate is known and respected within the group, the better.

When introduced to the "right" people, your goal should be to *connect* with them at a social level. Engage in friendly conversation. Ask more than you tell. Find out everything you can in the brief time you have with them.

- Listen for personal and professional connections, such as alumni of the same college, common friends and colleagues, shared hobbies and memberships in the same organizations. Use these connections as a reason to meet with them later—on a social level. You might be able to arrange that on the spot, or you can call them later.
- Listen for business and life changes that could have immediate or future financial implications. Note that information for when you meet with them later.
- Carry a small pocket-sized notebook (3-1/4″ × 4-1/2″) so you

can note *who*, *where* and *when* you met them, plus their phone number and *why* you should contact them later.

Also, think about ways to expand your own social network to meet new people. For example:

- Instead of turning down wedding invitations, attend every one you can. If possible, ask the host to seat you at the table with business and community leaders.
- Join a theater group, sporting club or hobby group composed of people you want to meet. Select ones that will hold your interest.
- Hold a tailgating cookout at a sporting event. Invite people you've met at other social events, and network with the groups around you.
- Explore the list of people who belong to your church, synagogue, theater group, sporting club or hobby group. Begin inviting those you want to meet to your home, or out for dinner or a drink.
- Teach a course, attend charitable fundraisers, participate in a walk-a-thon, attend a conference on a topic of interest to the affluent. The list is almost endless.

Community Groups

Community groups can expand your opportunities for connecting socially, but they add one other dimension that's even more important. Community groups emerge to serve a purpose, and people join to support what the group represents. The affluent who join community organizations often do so to give back to the community. They are drawn to other members who demonstrate a similar commitment through their participation in committees, events, fundraisers and other activities that advance the organization's purpose. This gives you an opportunity to *become one with the affluent* in very significant ways.

You may find a few members that you can approach on a business level when you first meet, but more often you'll need to first earn their trust. Your dedication to, and involvement in, the organization is the best way to do that. This requires you to involve yourself in activities that will ...

- Attract attention. Be dependable and available for responsibilities that increase your visibility—such as the chairperson of an event or committee.
- Enable you to relate to people on their interest level, and to build rapport through your relaxed, friendly manner.
- Earn their trust by listening to them, empathizing with their concerns, working alongside them, and giving—without calculating the potential gain.
- Offer an opportunity to use your organizational, leadership, and financial skills. However, don't volunteer for opportunities that require skills you don't have.

Make certain you . . .

- Seek out an *internal advocate* who can introduce you to key people and advise on business protocol—as suggested for social groups.
- Volunteer for fundraisers. There's no better way to show your commitment and use your financial skills on behalf of the organization.

Your focus should be on working alongside other members to build rapport, demonstrate your dependability and establish friendships. That's the wellspring from which your business opportunities will emerge.

You're already familiar with the best known types of community organizations.

- Alumni associations
- Chambers of commerce
- Charities
- Civic organizations
- Cultural organizations
- Economic clubs
- Fraternal organizations
- Hospitals and other medical charities
- Museums
- Professional organizations
- Social service charities

Because of the time and effort required to connect with community organization members, please select those organizations carefully. The following five questions will serve as a litmus test:

- Do the purpose and goals of this organization capture your interest? If not, it will be difficult to stay involved. Think about (or check into) the purpose behind each type of organization listed above. Which ones attract your interest?

- Do the group's activities and events attract affluent individuals? Some organizations have wealthy people on their rolls, but not at their functions.

- Does the organization provide opportunities to meet new people on (at minimum) a monthly basis? Some organizations schedule events two to four times a year, which is not often enough.

- Is this organization recognized as a positive contributor to the community? Avoid organizations that embroil themselves in controversial issues.

- Will your interests and expertise enable you to be an effective volunteer?

- Can you afford to be involved? Go beyond basic membership fees and check the typical cost of monthly meetings, special events and expected contributions to any fundraising activities.

Select carefully, participate wisely, and the rewards will come. You can establish significant relationships through many small involvements. And you can offer to provide professional expertise when an individual opens that window of opportunity—always suggesting a separate face-to-face meeting where "talking business" will be appropriate.

Industry Groups

This strategy is often referred to as *industry immersion*, and that's a good description of what will occur. There are several reasons why it's ideal for a Rainmaker to pursue industry groups.

- As a professional, it makes perfect sense to take special interest in an industry that you believe is vital to your area's economic development. It helps you become a knowledgeable advisor to your clients. Most people you contact within the industry will immediately see that connection.

- Key people within the industry, and companies you choose to target, will welcome your interest because of your professional link to investors. Many will want to make friends with you as much as you want to befriend them.
- Becoming connected to a corporate community will put you in direct contact with affluent prospects, resulting in new clients and referrals to their associates.
- Because this is a business environment, it often takes less time to "get down to business" with the people you contact—versus social and community groups. People are ready to talk business, and expect business relationships to emerge from those conversations.

Begin by contacting your Chamber of Commerce and other organizations that are leading economic development efforts in your area. Meet with individuals in those organizations who are personally connected to those efforts. You'll want to know two things . . .

- The *anchor industry(ies)* in your area—the one(s) considered to be at the heart of your community's economic future. When members mention an industry, ask why they believe that industry is a catalyst for economic development. Listen for such factors as shifting economic indicators, consumer preferences, innovation, regulatory changes, geopolitical realignment and anything else suggesting that a specific industry is a good choice.
- The *leading and emerging company(ies)* in that industry—the one(s) they believe will be at the forefront of the economic development effort. Again, ask why they selected each company. Listen for connections to the same factors mentioned when discussing the anchor industry(ies). You may discover that the largest company is not the industry leader, and especially not the emerging leader.

Choose an **industry** and the **company(ies)** in your area where you will begin your effort to connect with **key people**. Learn as much as you can, and meet as many key people as possible. Preparation is important. For each company selected, start here:

- Read the SEC filings on the company. This will provide key company information, including its name, address, telephone number, state of incorporation, Central Index Key (CIK) number, Standard Industrial Classification (SIC) code, fiscal year end, and other valuable information about problems, and how management plans to increase the company's value.

Each of the following provides an excellent way for you to connect with affluent decision-makers in the company(ies) you've selected. As a financial professional who has influence over people with substantial assets to invest, you will have their attention. In each case, your goal is to learn as much as you can, and to meet as many key people as possible.

1. **Arrange a Tour of Company Facilities.**

    This is an excellent way to meet key executives and learn vital inside information, but it's important that those introductions be arranged prior to your tour. You might be able to call the company's communications department and set up a tour, but that is not your best approach. You need an *internal advocate* who can help arrange the tour and convince someone high in the organization to be your guide, preferably the top executive at that facility. You need a tour guide who believes you're important enough to warrant 90 minutes of her valuable time.

    That internal advocate might be suggested by clients, family members, friends, colleagues or acquaintances. From your involvement in social and community groups, you may know (or know of) a key individual who works for, or serves on, the board of the company you've targeted, or who personally knows a senior executive. This is an important element of a successful company tour, so keep searching until you find the right person.

    Arrive on time. Chat for a few minutes to break the ice, and then tell your guide how eager you are to learn everything you can about the operation. See as much, and talk to as many key people, as you can.

As you talk with people, keep thinking about how you could help them find financial-related solutions to the issues they discuss. Look for openings to schedule a face-to-face meeting at their earliest convenience.

2. **Attend Industry Conferences.**

These events tend to attract ambitious people looking for new and important information relating to the theme of the conference, and it's these people that you want to meet. The fact that you're there and eager to learn will help you to build an affinity with them.

As you interact with attendees, ask about upcoming conferences (they will be impressed). Enter the words "conference" and the specific industry in your favorite Internet search engine to learn more about conferences they suggest—or to identify other conferences that might be of interest to you. Conference websites frequently list speakers and the companies that have booked display booth space. Research these speakers and companies to uncover information that will help you introduce yourself to the people you really want to know.

Book a room at the conference hotel, so you can spend time networking. While at the conference:

- Arrive early each day, and stay late. Attend every informal gathering you can find.
- Keep glancing at name badges. Introduce yourself to at least one person before, during and after each meeting. Make certain you are favorably remembered.
- Arrange to meet with key people for every meal.
- Sit near the front at every meeting, if possible, to make yourself visible. Ask financially-related questions when questions are invited—if you believe such questions will be interpreted by the audience as valid contributions. Avoid controversial questions!

- Take notes during every speech, especially from the speakers you want to contact later for additional information or networking purposes.
- Purchase conference audiotapes on topics involving industry trends that could pose investment opportunities. Then make certain you listen to them.

Spend the 30 days following the conference following up on the contacts you made. Begin within two to three days after returning home.

3. **Attend Annual Shareholder Meetings.**

These meetings are used to showcase the company, so management will be eager to impress any financial professional with the perceived ability to affect wealth. Also, people who may be otherwise difficult to reach will often be there.

Call the company's financial PR firm or internal communications staff to let them know you'll be attending. You should ask who they expect to attend and if there is any other information they would like you to know. Once you identify yourself as a financial advisor targeting the affluent who invest in companies like this one, they will probably want to meet you when you arrive and introduce you around. Make an appointment to meet the PR or communications person at a specific time.

If left alone at any point, introduce yourself to as many people as you can. Let them know who you are, what you do (your 10-second introduction), and why you're attending—which is to learn as much about the company as possible so you can better guide your client's investments. The key people you want to meet:

- Directors—especially those from outside the organization that you have targeted in advance.
- Chief Executive Officer (CEO), President, Chief Operating Officer (COO).
- Chief Financial Officer (CFO).

- Vice Presidents– especially Human Resources, Sales & Marketing, R&D and other key functions.
- Other outsiders who can connect you to people and money in motion. Examples are executives from other companies, top level consultants, college and university faculty and deans, executive search firms and venture capitalists.

These three efforts to immerse yourself in a vital industry will lead you to other introductions and referrals as well—to customers and suppliers of the companies where you're making inroads, and to the social and community groups to which key people in those companies are connected.

Strategic Referral Alliances

Not all referrals need come from satisfied clients. Many can come through strategic alliances you create with CPAs, attorneys and others. These alliances should be made with professionals who provide complementary, but non-competitive, products and services to the affluent people you wish to contact.

CPAs and attorneys are an excellent choice because they are the advisors the affluent tend to trust most. However, CPAs and attorneys will also be cautious about forming strategic relationships, so you need to offer more than a simple exchange of referrals. Your strategic alliances will result in good referrals, but they should be built on the financial expertise and products you can offer your partners to help them better serve their affluent clients. Whenever they have a financial-related question, you want them to call you first. That's the difference between a simple referral alliance and a strategic referral alliance.

You want to work with CPAs and attorneys who serve the types of clients you have targeted. Begin by identifying the information, services and products that would interest each group the most. Transform your list into a checklist that you can review with each CPA and attorney to determine their key interests.

Forget the yellow pages or any other listing of CPAs and attorneys in your area. Instead, ask your clients, family, friends, colleagues and acquaintances for their recommendations. If you're involved in social, community and/or industrial groups, you may already know the people you want to contact.

When you meet with a CPA or attorney (or any professional) to explore a strategic referral alliance, keep referrals out of the conversation until you have established three things:

- The value you can bring to the person's practice through the specific information, services and products identified as most important.
- You are a financial professional who works very hard to establish long-term relationships. Differentiate yourself from transactional brokers.
- You seek the same type of long-term relationship with your strategic partners.

When asked what you hope to receive from this relationship, answer:

- The opportunity to provide the services and products they identified when the opportunity arises.
- Introductions and referrals to people they believe you can serve well, and who match your *Ideal Affluent Targeted Prospect Profile*.

Approach each alliance as you would any professional relationship. Honor all commitments, and serve the other person well, adding value whenever possible. There are five keys to making your Strategic Referral Alliance strategy work:

- Serve your clients, alliance partners and referred prospects well. Provide true value that exceeds expectations. Nurture relationships of trust.
- Be clear about your *Ideal Affluent Targeted Prospect Profile*.
- Give generously, believing that the benefits will come.

- After you contact a referral, keep your strategic referral alliance partner fully informed of your progress with that prospect.
- Be the real deal!

Intimate Client Events

Intimate client events provide a specialized type of strategic interaction. However, it's important that you not lose sight of the primary purpose, which is showing your appreciation to your best clients.

By continually strengthening the loyalty of your best clients, you'll receive more solicited and unsolicited introductions to people with the potential to become Ideal Clients. Since affluent investors make most decisions through word-of-mouth influence, strategically crafted client appreciation events become a wonderful platform for stimulating that influence. Carefully choose the clients you invite, and the people you want them to invite to your events.

Many types of events can be used: a dinner, golf outing, personal growth seminar, barbecue—the list goes on. If you aren't certain about an event idea, ask your clients for opinions. Be guided by your clients' interests and your own imagination. The following example—of a dinner party—illustrates seven opportunities to express your appreciation before, during and after the event:

- The initial phone call to invite clients (and spouses).
- The confirmation letter sent to those who accept.
- The reminder phone call—two or three days before the event.
- The informal reception before the formal dinner.
- The dinner and the program that follows dinner.
- The informal mingling before everyone leaves.
- The follow-up phone call—two or three days following the event.

An intimate client event builds loyalty by making the client feel appreciated at each point of contact. Here are some tips on how to make that happen:

1. Plan two or three events for the next three to five months. Set the dates, book the facilities, and arrange the programs for all three—*before* you begin making calls for the first event. When you invite clients to the first event, you will have two later events they can attend if the first date doesn't work for them. You should start calling about three to four weeks before the first event. **Do not invite clients by letter!**

2. Limit the number of clients invited, and be sure to engage in a personal conversation with each client sometime during the event.

3. The confirming letter should include complete information on location and parking, plus an expression of your enthusiasm about their attendance.

4. Before the event, you and your team should plan to ensure that no one is ever left alone. Critical times include the informal reception before the official dinner or activities, and the informal mingling before everyone leaves. Make certain everyone will receive adequate attention at all times:

   • Set up a seating arrangement so that clients will be next to team members who know as much as possible about them and their families. If you plan to separate clients and their spouses, be sure the spouses are also sitting next to someone who knows as much as possible about them.

   • Assign each client and spouse to at least two team members who will keep an eye out for them during the informal reception and informal wrap-up. If a client or spouse is suddenly alone, someone should approach him or her immediately.

5. The quality of the location, dinner and activities won't be noticed by clients—unless any one of them is of *poor quality*. The location must be just right; the food must be wonderful and acceptable to everyone (i.e., don't forget vegetarians and others with special diets); and the program (30–40 minutes maximum) should be informative and entertaining for everyone.

Everything must say, "Because we appreciate you, we care enough to give you the very best."

6. Unless you have a very good reason to do otherwise, do not bring up business during the follow-up phone calls. Instead, offer a sincere "thanks for coming, we were honored by your presence" type of exchange. If you've already touched upon business topics with this individual, and want to reference it during your call, say something like:

> *I wanted to tell you how much we enjoyed having you at the dinner on Monday night. We were truly honored by your presence. Also, we have a quarterly review meeting scheduled for Friday at 3 P.M., and I wanted to make certain that was still OK with you.*

A well-planned and intimate client event leads to predictable behaviors—including the additional business and referrals that loyal clients provide.

In their efforts to become Rainmakers, some of our students initially complain that these high-impact methods don't produce as much impact as they'd like. What we've discovered, however, is that these students tend to treat the activities as simple extensions of the cold call—in other words, they're far too mechanical. When you cold call, you're performing a drill. When you engage in high-impact Rainmaker activities you're participating in a romance. You must be sincere. You really have to love it! Yes, it's still a numbers game, but Rainmakers recognize the importance of developing personal relationships amidst the ongoing execution of these activities.

When using high-impact prospecting methods, your objective is to get to know qualified prospects, get them to like you and respect your professional competence, and begin to establish trust. All of this is necessary before they'll be ready to "talk business." Once they reach that point, however, not only will they be ready for a long-term relationship, they may be ready to serve as an internal advocate.

Ask questions—lots of questions. Look for things you have in common. Search for ways to become involved in activities and events that interest them. Find ways to help and support them. Most of all: be patient.

As the relationship evolves, they will discover what you do and begin thinking about how this relates to their needs, and the needs of people important to them. At the same time, you will also uncover those needs, and determine when the time is right to approach them on a professional level.

Rainmakers understand this, and that's why these methods have such high impact.

SUMMARY

High-impact activities must be executed the right way, to the right prospect, for the right reasons. This requires both planning and skill— strategy and tactics. It makes no sense to perform high-impact activities without maximizing their value.

Mastering the art of introductions and referrals is essential for a Rainmaker, which is why I cover these activities again in Chapter 8. Strategic networking, social groups, community groups and industry groups each offer unique opportunities. Make certain that you carefully target your involvement in whatever group(s) you choose to pursue your *Ideal Client Profile,* and don't make the mistake of spreading yourself too thin. Join groups for which you have enough time and interest to become an active participant.

Intimate client events are an excellent method of thanking your best clients while conducting strategic prospecting. Be sure to follow the steps outlined above, because these events are a goldmine when executed properly. If not, they're simply a client appreciation event.

Always pay attention to how you execute these high-impact activities. Little things mean a lot.

> ### Research Facts
>
> ▶ 72% of our survey respondents brought in new clients by asking for introductions.
>
> ▶ 78% of our survey respondents brought in new clients by networking (all forms).
>
> ▶ 90% of our survey respondents brought in new clients by asking for referrals.

TAKING ACTION

- Select on organization—social, community or industry—to join as an active member. If you already belong to an organization, become more active.
- Research other organizations to determine if any would make a good fit.
- Schedule one intimate client event.
- Add one name per day to your Top 25 Introduction Notebook.

7

Minimize Low-Impact Activities

Only 27% of respondents brought in new clients using either direct mail or cold calling.

—Factoid, 2005 ANAC Research

Note that I've used the word "minimize"—not eliminate. There's no question that direct-response advertising, telemarketing, Internet marketing and public relations (among others) are invaluable tools for attracting and retaining customers. In fact, some industries thrive on the power of a single marketing vehicle (e.g., most magazines rely on direct-mail for new subscriptions and renewals). In the abstract, no one sales or marketing tool is superior to another. When selling high-end services to affluent consumers, however, only three activities cut the mustard:

- Targeted Networking.
- Introductions.
- Referrals.

With the exception of targeted seminars (a moderate-impact activity), everything else is a low-impact prospecting method that deserves a lower priority. In general, low-impact activities should be used to supplement your "heavy artillery," not as a substitute.

Don't get me wrong, supplements *can* add value. If you have the money, a good public relations agency can boost your credibility and visibility using press releases, ghostwritten books and articles. A well-designed direct-response vehicle *will* raise awareness of who you are and what you offer. What's more, most prospects *expect* to take home your professionally written, 16-page, four-color brochure after the first meeting. But Rainmakers don't let "old school" marketing tools distract them from their "critical path"—the road to close relationships with ideal prospects.

Suicide by PR

Jeremy was a would-be Rainmaker who abandoned the critical path for what he thought was an easier route. It was a shortcut to disaster.

Jeremy founded and chaired a non-profit organization dedicated to helping older women plan for their retirements. Although the organization was partially funded by a university in New York State, Jeremy needed more funding to achieve his goal of reaching women nationwide. In the beginning, he played it smart, and was a tireless fundraiser. He hired a public relations firm to generate publicity, which he used to establish his credentials among the movers and shakers of Fortune 500 corporations. He staged events to raise awareness, attended parties, and met with any influential person who'd give him the time of day. It paid off.

Within a year, Jeremy had enough money to stage numerous seminars and even produce a "professional" how-to video on pre-retirement planning. He was starting to get the word out.

Unfortunately, Jeremy was also getting tired, burning out from the fast pace of so much face-to-face. He should have taken a long vacation or leave of absence. Instead, he effectively cancelled his relationship-building efforts, and decided to fund the non-profit from sales of the how-to video. To accomplish this, he hired a new public relations firm to generate sales from publicity alone. The head of that PR firm, now a friend, describes what happened next.

"First of all, we were *not* told that he'd severed ties to his corporate sponsors. Second, we were informed that the video would be sold through both retail outlets and direct mail—that our media relations campaign was just the opening salvo of a much larger bombardment.

We got him spots on local radio, in national magazines—even a feature segment on CNBC. Based on the publicity alone, he received something like 800 calls from buyers—people who went out of their way to call the number listed in the magazine stories or who telephoned radio and television stations asking how to order.

"Then Jeremy dropped the bomb on us. There *never was* a retail or direct-mail strategy. We were it. By some miracle, our PR campaign was supposed to generate tens of thousands of orders. I wanted to kill him . . . but I felt too sorry for him. Between our fees and the video producer's, he had no money left. If he'd been upfront about his 'master plan,' my partner and I would have told him it was *suicide*."

A dramatic case? Yes, but by no means unique.

The Silver Bullet

I'm regularly approached by prospective clients who want me to make them magnetic—to wave my magic wand, and cause prospects to gravitate toward them like the moons of Jupiter. I tell these prospects what I said in Chapter 1. There is no silver bullet to becoming a Rainmaker. There is no secret. All it takes is discipline—the mindset that says, "I will perform the activities and develop the skills needed to reach my goals."

It's like losing weight. You can try every fad diet ever published, or you can decide to get serious by eating right and exercising. The key is willpower.

Shortcuts rarely succeed—especially in the affluent markets. Think about it. Would you hand over $1 million to a financial advisor because he has a "cool" website? Would your corporation hire a law firm to design tax shelters because one of its partners received favorable mention in the state bar's newsletter?

I wouldn't. I might initiate contact with a company based on the strength of its direct-mail brochure, but ad copy alone won't determine my final decision.

Remember, affluent consumers are highly skeptical of traditional sales and marketing techniques. For that reason, they tend to conduct thorough online and offline research before making a major purchase decision. In addition, they rely on trusted friends and associates for advice, and they ask LOTS of questions. Finally, they make final decisions based on the quality of your personal attention, as well as their perceptions of your competence and trustworthiness. You can't stuff these qualities into an envelope or e-mail.

Low-Impact Activities—Pros and Cons

I won't bother to discuss cold calling here, because the tactic is completely inappropriate for affluent prospects. The affluent don't like unsolicited calls, and they don't make time for them. Like most Americans, they rate telemarketing as one notch below wrong numbers and obscene callers. Even if you penetrate the usual "firewalls" –caller ID and personal secretaries—the most you can reasonably expect is a request for additional (written) information.

General Advertising	*Pros:* Sustained print and broadcast advertising raises awareness, raises your profile, and helps you create and define positive images, positioning and branding for your service package(s). In addition, general advertising can reach huge numbers of prospective buyers.
	Cons: Aside from being extremely expensive, it's difficult to scientifically measure the number of leads generated. Most of your money is wasted reaching people other than your targeted prospects, and—when it comes to affluent prospects—few (if any) will decide to purchase from you because of your magazine ads or television commercials.
Direct Mail	*Pros:* Allows you to test and refine your messages, strategies and offers before rolling out.

Prospects can be more accurately targeted, and the results scientifically measured.

Cons: Costs of acquiring mailing lists, copy-writing, design, printing and distribution can be enormous. Response rates in the low single-digits are par for the course, and most of those who do respond will be less affluent and less sophisticated. At best, your mail package may prompt some prospects to contact you for a meeting, but it will never close the sale.

Email

Pros: Same as for direct mail.

Cons: Production and distributions costs are negligible, but response rates—and the image you project by using this approach—are much lower. It's even easier to delete unsolicited e-mail than to throw away physical junk mail. Spam is considered sleazy (because it is), which is not the impression you want as a Rainmaker.

Publicity

Pros: News and feature stories can generate awareness of who you are and what you offer, and provide *implied* third-party endorsement. Clippings and audio/video excerpts can be excellent supplements to sales materials and presentations.

Cons: Media relations, marketing communications and other publicity efforts are designed to raise awareness and enhance credibility, not to generate leads. You have no direct control over the messages featured in any news or feature story, and cannot target your audiences.

Books & Articles

Pros: Whether self-written or ghostwritten, books and articles are designed to enhance your credibility as an expert in your field. Depending on the quality of the information you provide, and the nature and scope of distribution, these tools can help you achieve "guru" status.

Cons: Join the club. Thirty years ago, only the more sophisticated professionals supplemented their marketing with articles designed for consumer and/or trade publications. These days, it's hard to find someone who hasn't. And, with the advent of online outsourcing and publishing on demand (POD), it's easier—and cheaper—than ever to hire qualified ghostwriters and to get your book "published." The result: online bookstores and company websites are flooded with mediocre "me-to" books designed for no other purpose than to build the "author's" reputation. How many prospects are actually reading these books and e-books is anyone's guess.

Your Website   See Chapter 10.

Seminars and Workshops

Seminars and workshops have long been a staple of financial planners targeting the middle-class and near-affluent. But there's no reason why service providers outside the financial services industry cannot employ them. And there's no reason not to target the affluent. I know two estate-planning attorneys who have become magnets for affluent clients by conducting *the right seminars for the right people.*[7]

Jerry conducts a free, three-hour seminar every month for affluent people to help them understand the value and timing issues related to estate planning. What began as an evening class at a community college has evolved into a targeted seminar because Jerry realized that by

---

[7] Ibid.

providing information free of any sales pitch, the people he wanted to reach became convinced of his integrity and sincerity. Also, the more his clients understood about estate planning when they asked for help, the better clients they became. Jerry doesn't solve individual estate issues during the workshop, but he does provide enough information for attendees to determine whether their current estate plan (if they have one) is adequate. The odds are on his side, because most estate plans were developed by attorneys who do not specialize in estate planning.

Harry, who is also an estate-planning attorney, takes a different approach. Although he works only with an affluent clientele, all of his business comes through referrals from financial advisors and financial planners. Therefore, Harry considers those financial professionals who continually refer business to him as his first-tier clients.

To position himself as a go-to attorney for complex estate work, Harry conducts workshops at local association meetings, statewide events, national meetings, and even for a couple of major financial services companies. As far as Harry is concerned, conducting a workshop at a national meeting is a good use of his time because he is educating financial professionals to become more "judicious" in selecting who they use for their clients. He knows that anyone "who has earned a JD degree and then gets some estate-planning software can develop an estate plan and charge $5,000." So part of his mission is to educate his clients (financial professionals) on some of the basic intricacies of complex estate planning. He even teaches them which red flags to look for in estate plans that have already been done.

In his own market, Harry offers an open invitation to any financial professional interested in learning more about estate issues. He even gets them to buy lunch. He has positioned himself to be both the affluent client's advocate and the financial professional's strategic resource. That has made Harry truly magnetic. One hundred percent of his business comes from introductions and referrals from professionals within the financial services industry.

Harry and Jerry have successfully employed workshops and seminars—moderate impact activities—to become literal money magnets. But they've done so by recognizing that these activities are just a springboard to high-impact prospecting methods. The work doesn't end when the lights come up and the Q&A is finished. It's only just begun. Now it's time to proactively encourage comprehensive, one-on-one meetings with interested attendees. Now it's time to put their face-to-face skills to the test.

Unfortunately, many service providers transform this moderate-impact activity into a low-impact waste of time. After securing the high-school auditorium, they place ads in local newspapers inviting everyone in town to attend a Tuesday-evening seminar entitled "Choosing the Right Mutual Fund" or "Life Insurance for Dummies." After a generic presentation and tedious Q&A, most attendees flee—bored and hoping to catch an episode of *CSI* before it's too late. A handful of stragglers stay behind to ask for free advice, and accept business cards and brochures. Most likely, the service provider will never see any of these people again—outside of a supermarket checkout line.

Do your homework. Target your seminars and workshops to the right people with the right information. Otherwise, you may as well volunteer to teach a class in astrology at the nearest Learning Annex.

Below Low-Impact

As I was writing this book, I received a call from a prospect—someone who'd spent lots of money with one of my coaching competitors. After complaining about the program he'd just finished, he asked if I could help him. "I hope you're not just going to ask me to penetrate my key clients, yada, yada, yada," he said.

Apparently, his previous advisors had suggested that everyone form strategic alliances with the CPAs in their area. Instead of developing relationships with CPAs for the eventual purpose of getting referrals, however, he was told to ask the CPAs how he could help them grow their businesses.

This strategy has merit—if it's properly executed by an expert in this field, one who can truly add value to a CPA's practice. Otherwise, this was probably one of the most foolish prospecting activities this individual could have been doing. Since when did this financial advisor become a business consultant? Does he have a background in practice management? What qualifies him to help a CPA run his practice? Why would he position himself to do this? The sad reality is that by pretending to be something that he wasn't, my caller had severely damaged his credibility within the CPA community. Ouch!

Fortunately, the prospect agreed with my assessment, but liked the idea of writing another book. (He'd already had two books ghostwritten.) Here's my take: unless you can write a book, unless you have information for a book that's unique and balanced, your audience isn't interested or impressed. Who wants to read another book about "the 7 Steps to Smart Investing" written by—who?—another stockbroker? Hundreds of brokers are hiring hundreds of ghostwriters to produce these tomes. The result: zip, nada, nothing.

This prospect bragged that he'd hired a ghostwriter to write a column for a local newspaper. When I asked him what had happened, I learned that—you guessed it—*nothing had happened*. No inquiries, no leads, no clients—no results.

"There's a fly in your ointment," I said. "There's a big disconnect. You've been in a major market for 18 years, and you don't have any centers-of-influence that you're confident in approaching. That's hard to believe. And now you're talking to accountants, and presenting yourself as a business consultant who's going to help them grow their business, to create a strategic alliance, so hopefully, they'll give you referrals. And you've had a couple of books written for you. This makes no sense.

"How do you demonstrate your value to prospects and clients? What do your clients say about you when they talk with a family member or a peer? How do you exceed client expectations? Do you provide Ritz Carlton service with FedEx efficiency?"

His response was basically, "duh?"

What was this Rainmaker wannabe looking for? He was looking to buy his way into being a magnet for the affluent. He wanted to build his practice by pretending to be somebody he wasn't. Not only is this disingenuous (at best), many people would say it's dishonest. In addition, it's just plain stupid. Looking for magic, searching for that elusive golden key without rolling up your sleeves and working to become the real deal is bad business.

All or Nothing

You can't be a part-time rainmaker. It requires total commitment. You have to work hard to be the real deal, work smart by engaging in the high-impact activities, and work hard at continually refining your Rainmaking skills. This level of commitment requires more than simply liking your job. You have to *love* it! You must represent something that you absolutely believe in, because if you don't believe in it, you'll be found out. Each activity discussed in this chapter has a deserved place in the business world—including strategic alliances, cross-promotions, contests, bottom-of-receipt promotions, etc., etc. But in the world of affluent selling, only three methods make the grade.

Rainmaker Activities focus on *what to do*. In the next section, we will focus on Rainmaker Skills, which is *how to do it*. This is a good time to assess your own Rainmaking skill level. Although you've already worked through a Rainmakers' Activity Profile in Chapter 5, please bear with me, because I want you to assess these specific high-impact activities within the context of the skills required to be successful. I will explain my logic more clearly after you have completed this Skill/Activity Assessment.

For each of the statements in Chart 6, there are two sets of questions. Circle YES or NO for each set: (1) Skill Level—knowing what to do and how to do it; and (2) doing it consistently.

If you're like most of our rainmaker pupils, you circled "Yes" a lot more under the heading *Knowing What & How* than you did under *Doing it Consistently.* Why? Because most Rainmaker wannabes assume that they already know *what* to do, and therefore, they think that they know *how* to do it. Because these activities are so basic, it's easy to assume you already possess the skills—especially if you're not actively in the rainmaking mode. This is especially true for veterans, and it's a BIG mistake.

Here's the same question I ask our students after they complete this

Chart 6		
Rainmaker Activity & Skills Self-Assessment		
	SKILL LEVEL Knowing What & How	**ACTIVITY** Doing It Consistently
1. Finding affluent prospects?	Yes No	Yes No
2. Proactively asking for and getting referrals to affluent prospects?	Yes No	Yes No
3. Proactively asking for and getting introductions to affluent prospects?	Yes No	Yes No
4. Constantly networking to place your-self in the path of affluent prospects?	Yes No	Yes No
5. Getting face-to-face with affluent prospects?	Yes No	Yes No
6. Effectively connecting with affluent prospects?	Yes No	Yes No
7. Building rapport so affluent prospects can quickly determine that they 'like and trust' you?	Yes No	Yes No
8. Developing professional respect in the minds of affluent prospects?	Yes No	Yes No
9. Overcoming objections and affluent skepticism of salespeople?	Yes No	Yes No
10. Convincing an affluent prospect to conduct business with you?	Yes No	Yes No

assessment. Even if you circled "Yes," and think you know what to do regarding a particular activity, if you're not doing that activity with any degree of consistency, what is the probability that you might need to brush-up on your skills in that area? To a person, I receive universal agreement with the need to brush-up. If you aren't consistently doing high-impact rainmaking activities, you need to roll-up your sleeves and work on your skills. Period!

This exercise is one of the reasons Rainmakers are so few and far between. Firms are not teaching these skills, and a good part of the reason is because the majority of their salespeople assume they already have them.

SUMMARY

Minimize, but don't eliminate, moderate and low-impact activities such as seminars and workshops, direct-response advertising and public relations. These "old school" marketing tools are no substitute for high-impact prospecting activities, but they can be valuable supplements. In general, lower-impact activities generate awareness of who you are and what you have to offer, and may cause prospects to initiate "first contact," but that's as far as they go. Use them wisely and efficiently—as springboards to higher-impact methods. Never rely on marketing gurus touting unusual strategies. Most of these machinations produce results that are far below low-impact.

You cannot buy your way into Rainmaking. You must be the real deal, and you must make a total commitment to becoming the real deal. This requires work. Whether it is expanding your knowledge, revising your activities, working on your skills, or some combination of the aforementioned, time and effort are required.

Research Facts

▶ Only 27% of ANAC Survey respondents brought in new clients using direct mail.

▶ Only 27% of ANAC Survey respondents brought in new clients by cold calling.

▶ Only 40% of ANAC Survey respondents brought in new clients by conducting seminars.

▶ Rainmakers concentrate their efforts on the high-impact activities.

TAKING ACTION

- If you are considering developing (or refining) a targeted seminar or workshop, your first step is to determine who would be your best audience, and where you could conduct such an event. What kinds of topics would appeal to your ideal clients or major centers-of-influence?
- How much effort are you dedicating to low-impact vs. high-impact prospecting activities? Over a six-week period, track your hours to gauge where your time is being spent.
- Eliminate any low-impact prospecting activities, unless you have an unusual situation and they are generating quality face-time with affluent prospects.
- Commit to becoming a full-time Rainmaker.
- Identify the high-impact activities you need to use, and commit to performing at least one high-impact activity every day.
- Identify the skills you need to work on.
- Assess your deliverables, and make absolutely certain that you are the real deal!

The Right Skills

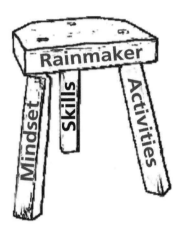

8

Handling the Face-to-Face

For me, the most shocking revelation from the 2005 ANAC survey was the intense resistance and reluctance among many financial advisors to do what it takes to succeed. Despite all of the technical platforms provided by their companies—wealth management tools, investment products, banking services, etc.—a significant number of advisors simply do not want to perform the activities of a Rainmaker.

Too many people hide behind jargon and a façade of expertise. Maybe that's why the financial services industry has dispensed so many new titles in recent years—financial advisor, wealth manager, senior vice president of asset allocation, etc. Titles are fine, but they don't replace the activities. In addition, many professionals simply talk too much, without saying anything. While the true Rainmaker builds relationships by asking strategic questions *and really listening*, the Rainmaker wannabe tries to impress prospects with multi-syllabic jargon to demonstrate how much he or she knows.

Chart 7		
Survey Respondents Who Added ZERO New Clients		
Targeted Investable Asset Level	**Those EAGER To Prospect**	**Those Reluctant To Prospect**
$1 million and higher	9%	60%
$500,000 to $1 million	17%	44%
$250,000 to $500,000	14%	27%

This produces two outcomes:

1. The affluent prospect walks away thinking, "That was painful. This guy's really impressed with himself."
2. The Rainmaker wannabe walks away with absolutely NO INTELLIGENCE on the prospect—the very opposite of what he should have done.

If you're serious about becoming a Rainmaker, the good news is that it won't take long to distance yourself from your competition. On the other hand, be aware that even those who "walk the talk" frequently stumble. They make mistakes that could be easily avoided, as you are about to discover.

Barry's Story

After diligently engaging in high-impact Rainmaking activities, Barry found himself face-to-face with an affluent prospect in the lobby of an upscale hotel. Both he and the prospect were attending a silent auction fundraiser. This is how Barry recalled the high-impact face-to-face. . .

"We engaged in typical rapport-building small talk. After a few minutes, this affluent prospect asked me, 'What actually do you do?' I responded by pulling my new brochure out of the small leather carrying case I had with me, and handed it to my prospect. Mind you, this was not just a typical brochure. It was a beautiful $16,000 piece that I got for half price. A good client of mine is a partner in the advertising firm that created it, and I got a good deal.

My affluent prospect perused it rather quickly, commented that it was an 'impressive piece,' and placed it on the coffee table in front of us. He then looked me in the eye and asked, 'Why should I conduct business with you?' I was a taken aback, but I quickly recovered, suggesting that he actually 'read' the brochure.

The prospect picked up my brochure, thumbed through it quickly, placed it down again on the coffee table, and said in a firm tone, 'I don't read brochures. Just talk to me. Explain why I should consider doing business with you.' Now I was completely out of my element. The prospect had gained complete control of this high-impact encounter, and I was stumbling for words. Feeling very uncomfortable, I started thumbing through my own brochure. Then it got even worse.

As I began to read, this prospect asked to see the brochure again. I handed it to him, and he tore it into four pieces saying, 'This is what I think of brochures! If you can't talk straight to me, there obviously is nothing to talk about.' He got up and left."

Wow! Barry was doing many things right. He engaged in a high-impact networking activity, his Rainmaker Antennae were out, but he embarrassed himself. He simply lacked the skills to handle the face-to-face encounter. Barry was counting on his "impressive" brochure to do it for him. But as Barry learned—the hard way—*he* is the product.

Listen and Learn

In your first meeting with the prospect, you must ask questions that will enable you to gather information and develop rapport. You have to listen and learn so you can consider ways to provide real value to this person before attempting to discuss business, much less present your brochure.

The typical financial planner goes through a basic drill when meeting with a prospect. He takes total control (or so he thinks), and spends most of the time talking about himself, his products and services, how he delivers these products and services, and how professional and credible he is. In effect, he talks too much, listens too little, and fails to develop the skills necessary to begin transitioning this individual from a prospect to a client. All too frequently, like Barry, people lead with their brochures (albeit they aren't usually $16,000 brochures). Without making an effort to really know your prospect, there's no way you can position yourself as a solutions provider, a true professional who can add real value.

When you ask and listen in order to develop rapport, you really get to know a prospect. Say, for example, you discover that your prospect has an ill mother, and a sister who's about to lose her job. You can now talk about cash flow and suggest investments accordingly. You'll discover a wide range of likes and dislikes. You'll learn that this particular affluent prospect, Mr. Oechsli, really enjoys cowboy boots because he attended school in the Southwest. Knowing this, you decide to send him a picture book of cowboy boots that you recall seeing in an airport. Thanks to Amazon.com, you are able to track down this unique book and have it delivered to your prospect, complete with a note from you. Imagine Mr. Oechsli's surprise and delight at receiving this simple, but thoughtful, gift.

As a Rainmaker, you should always be thinking about the "coffee table book." What unique gift can you send to your prospect/client? To answer that question, you must learn enough about Mr. Oechsli to know he's a die-hard Atlanta Braves fan, went to school in Arizona, owns eight pairs of cowboy boots and a custom-made cowboy hat, and that he's an avid reader of history. Any one of those interests may warrant the gift of a "coffee table book" with a personal note attached. It could really make a difference, because it's personal!

Many of these same skills apply to your best clients as well. Remember that each of your top 25 clients should be responsible for six new clients over the course of your professional relationship. Call the client on her birthday, even if it's Sunday. Most people think they're beating the competition when they have an assistant mail a load of birthday cards. A Rainmaker is always personal. And, of course, each client will receive your cell phone number and 24/7 access to your time. Right?

A Rainmaker provides real service, not lip service. Whenever possible, you should under-promise and over-deliver. Whatever you do, *never* over-promise. More people get themselves into jams by over-promising than almost anything else.

Learn to ask the right questions. Learn to listen.

When it comes your time to talk, don't "pull a Barry" and whip out your brochure. Don't tell the prospect everything you've ever learned about XYZ. Instead, maintain a conversational tone while you ask questions. Then use the answers to introduce your services.

One Rainmaker starts with, "We work with a select group of families in the Chicago area, overseeing and coordinating their financial affairs. And we do it very carefully. We have to first make a thorough assessment of the client's financial state of affairs, and see if there's anything we can assist with. The second step is to profile everybody in advance to see if there's going to be a fit. And we insist upon everybody profiling us too. We want you to check us out, lift up the hood, kick the tires. If there's something we can help you with, if there's a fit, then there's a possibility we can have a working relationship."

The above creates a word picture about the Rainmaker's business that doesn't require braggadocio. In addition, he's applying some reverse psychology. By saying, "We have to profile everybody to see if there's a fit," he's suggesting that the prospect might not qualify. The implication is, "We never talk anybody into doing business with us." This takes a high degree of skill, and demonstrates why this person is a Rainmaker.

Watch for Red Flags

Telling the prospect that you want to make sure there's a fit isn't just clever psychology. It's also for your own protection. Your first meeting should serve as a screening tool—not just for the prospect, but for you. Keep your eyes peeled for red flags! A rainmaker watches for any number of warnings indicating that the prospect won't make a good client.

For instance, some prospects will harbor unrealistic expectations of what you can and cannot do. Recently, a friend told me that his sister wanted to live off her $100,000 inheritance for the rest of her life. She informed her financial planner that she expected an annual return on her investments of 20%. Good luck.

Others need so much hand-holding that you'll end up devoting too much time to people who produce only a small fraction of your income. One attorney spent several hours each day fielding calls from elderly clients. Following is a snippet from an actual (one-sided) conversation that his secretary overheard:

"How can I help you today, Mr. Renfield? It's me—Mr. Jameson. I'm your attorney. Your attorney! What do I . . . You called me! Yes, I

updated that yesterday. I mailed the forms to your home. They're in the mail. I just put the forms in the mail! I . . . I'm with another client right now. OK, I'll drop by with them after work. I'll come to see you after work!"

Most important, beware the prospect who demands to know what you charge. "What's your fee; what's your fee; what do you charge?" A Rainmaker, if at all possible, will never discuss price with an unsold prospect—never. Instead, she shifts seamlessly and says, "Before I can answer that question, we need to have a clear picture of your goals and what we need to do to make certain you achieve those goals. First, I have to thoroughly analyze your financial status to see if we can help. Second, we have to see if there's going to be a fit. We want you to profile us, and we'll profile you." The conversation continues from there, but this is a simple example of the requisite skills you need to develop in order to become a true Rainmaker.

Don't get sucked into quoting prices. I've watched even seasoned professionals fall into this trap dozens of times. Most of the financial advisors who get sucked into price discussions do so because they haven't learned how to position themselves as legitimate financial coordinators. They're unsure of their Rainmaker abilities, and basically view themselves as practitioners—a financial planner, an advisor, an investor of money or whatever. For a Rainmaker—true go-to financial coordinator—pricing is not centered around the cost of the products you recommend or your service fees. It involves establishing a reasonable fee for the bundle of products and services required to achieve your client's goals and create the future they desire. It includes unlimited meetings, access and advice from you. It is measured by the value you add to their lives—and by showing them what they will risk by not having you as their chief financial officer.

It's when advisors present themselves as financial-product-and-service providers that they get caught up in price tags and price tag comparisons.

Proving Your Competence

As a Rainmaker, you must have the skills to demonstrate your competence without coming off as a jargon-spewing know-it-all. You want to demonstrate your expertise in a casual, conversational way. If you really know your stuff (and you'd better), you must learn how to present that knowledge so that anyone with a 12th grade education can understand.

If you've successfully developed rapport, you now know something about the other person. You've done your homework before the meeting, listened and learned during the meeting, and gathered enough "intel" (Chapter 10 will cover "intel gathering" in more detail, using the Internet). Now you're positioned to probe deeper, and let the individual talk about his/her favorite subjects—themselves, their successes and their goals.

As you develop rapport, they discover reasons to like you, and the process of building trust begins. Trust has to be earned over time, so you're just initiating the process. But you initiate the process by being sincere and engaging.

Most of all, you are proving your competency by the seamless nature of your sales skills. When it's your turn to speak, you're able to create a simple and succinct word picture about what you do and how you can help them create the future they want.

Closing the Sale

Although a Rainmaker is never timid about asking for the business, she never asks for it prematurely. She waits until she's earned that emotional equity, until she's accrued some professional respect after demonstrating her competence. Only then will she say, "Brian, I'd like the opportunity to be your trusted financial coordinator" or "Brian, I'd like to talk business with you." Sometimes, she'll simply say, "Let's get started."

Whenever there's an objection, she stops, goes back, and addresses the issue directly. At this point, she might realize that she needs to develop a better rapport, or that she hasn't been clear enough. But she will be persistent. She's not going to let an opportunity get away without a fight. The Rainmaker is an expert at closing the deal, but she doesn't make it complicated. She keeps it simple.

What If I Have ZERO Sales Ability?

In my opinion, there's no such human being. If there were, his or her only hope for survival in the legal and financial worlds would be to work for a Rainmaker. He or she would have to live in the backroom— as an associate, an analyst or a researcher. In most cases, it's not that people lack the ability. They're just afraid to undertake face-to-face activities, so they claim to have no aptitude for sales. This was Jason's problem.

Jason is an excellent money manager, a CFA (Certified Financial Analyst) and MBA who comes from very intellectual stock. Although he's an athlete—and something of a tough guy—he's also very introverted. Jason has done well for himself, but has always hired junior people to be his "Rainmakers." As you may have guessed, these people always failed.

I was frustrated with Jason, and he was frustrated with himself. He knew he should be getting more business, and wondered why his employees couldn't produce. I slammed my hand on the table, and said, "You're doing this whole thing backwards. YOU need to be the Rainmaker." There was dead silence.

Aware that I was jeopardizing the jobs of two employees, I added, "You need to be the Kingpin Rainmaker. Your junior people can support your activities, but anything they bring into your practice is gravy. You're never going to grow to your potential if you don't have the guts to step up to the plate. This is not rocket science; it's about courage. You need to be able to sit down and ask your good clients for referrals. You need to get out there again, and play golf [he'd stopped because he was too busy managing money]."

To his credit, Jason followed my advice and began asking for introductions. He also joined a country club for $30,000, and started playing golf again. Since then, Jason has brought nearly $70 million into his business. He's still managing the money, but he's pulled his head out of the sand. His junior partners lasted three more months before they proved their worthlessness. They'd been blowing smoke while convincing Jason to spend money on brochures and other materials to support their half-hearted efforts.

This is only one case, but it demonstrates that *anyone* who wants to become a Rainmaker can become a Rainmaker. It takes commitment, courage, high-impact activities, and skill. To his credit, Jason immediately became engaged in the high-impact rainmaking activities, and I continued to coach him until he mastered the necessary skills. Most people don't have the mindset or the courage to take that ego risk. They're very good at what they do, but they end up becoming knowledge workers for Rainmakers.

SUMMARY

There is no substitute for skill training. (At the time of this writing, Tiger Woods is still working with his swing coach Hank Haney.) You must pay close attention to developing the necessary skills of Rainmaker. There's nothing worse than being embarrassed like Barry. Could he have mastered these skills? Absolutely! But, he first needed to get his ego out of the way, accept that he was a salesperson, admit he needed to improve his sales skills, and then work at mastering them. Whether or not he had a $16,000 brochure is irrelevant. With the proper skill set, he could have successfully used whatever collateral material was at hand.

Many service providers are very reluctant to do what it takes to bring in affluent clients, but even those who "walk the talk" are liable to stumble. Because they don't know any better, many people get tangled up in their own jargon, trying too hard to impress their prospects, when they should be asking, listening, gathering information and developing a rapport. By really listening to what the person says about his personal and business life—about his likes and dislikes—you position yourself to provide better service and value. That includes small gifts, birthday greetings and other "personal touches."

In your first meeting, it's important to demonstrate your competency, while also screening the prospect. Watch for red flags, and never talk price with an unsold prospect. And if an unexpected opportunity to close surfaces, don't be afraid to ask for the business. There's no such thing as someone with no sales ability. If you doubt that, spend a couple of hours watching a four-year-old "sell" his mother. At a young age, kids are born salespeople. They're always asking for the order, and they rarely take "no" for an answer. As we mature into adulthood, we must capture that same spirit as we continually work on our skills.

Research Facts

▶ 60% of respondents who were reluctant to prospect added ZERO new clients with investable assets of $1 million or more.

▶ Only 29% of respondents who were eager to prospect added ZERO new clients with investable assets of $1 million or more.

TAKING ACTION

- Make an effort to learn as much as possible about a prospect you are targeting. Ask your center-of-influence or introduction source, or conduct a Google search (see Chapter 10).
- Use your background information to carefully ask questions and build rapport.
- The more a prospect perceives that you are interested in what she has accomplished, the more quickly she will like and trust you.
- During an initial face-to-face, always be thinking about the "coffee table book" you're going to send. This will force you to ask the

right questions and really get to know your prospect. Send the gift whenever appropriate (not all first encounters warrant a book).

- Create a written word picture of what you do, and the services you provide.
- Rehearse the word picture with friends, colleagues or family members. Have them ask tough questions afterward to help you prepare responses.
- Practice your questions, outline your encounter, and be clear about your objective.
- Schedule another meeting and close the sale.

9

Refine Your Rainmaking Skills

Because the salesperson is the product, he or she has a major impact on making or breaking the sale.

—Factoid, 2004 APD Research

The Rainmaker stool is delicately balanced on its three legs:

- Mindset—knowing what to do.
- Activity—doing it.
- Skill—knowing how and when to do it.

Rainmaking skills are *interpersonal skills* that require a blend of common sense, courtesy and finely tuned antennae.

Consider the following scenario. One of your clients knows a college grad who enjoys golf. The client asks if the young man can play along sometime, and you readily agree. On the day of the outing, the kid is incredibly polite and helpful, giving you pointers, raking the sand traps, holding the flags, etc. He's a pleasure.

What would a Rainmaker do next?

In the real-world case, the actual Rainmaker (Tom) was so impressed with the young man that he sent a handwritten thank-you note to the wealthy father, complimenting him on his son. Obviously, that Rainmaking activity needs to be followed up, which Tom will certainly do. He'll find a reason to get face-to-face with the father, which will probably involve another trip to the golf course.

What would Greg (Rainmaker wannabe) do?

First, Greg would have found a reason *not* to go golfing with his client in the first place. Second, he'd be reluctant to let an unknown kid play along, since the young man isn't an ideal affluent prospect. And even if Greg learned that the young man's father was a person of considerable wealth, it wouldn't occur to him to send a handwritten note to the father. He'd never think of reaching out to the father through the son.

Why wouldn't these thoughts occur to Greg? Two reasons: (1) he hasn't performed the right activities often enough to develop the proper mindset (he hasn't activated his Rainmaker's Achievement Cycle); and (2) the skills needed to execute the right activities fall outside his comfort zone. Tom wasn't entirely comfortable with sending the follow-up note either, but he ploughed ahead anyway. That's true of any Rainmaker. If you wait until you feel comfortable—if you wait until your confidence grows—you'll wait forever.

For many people, lack of confidence and comfort stem from feeling intimidated around wealthy people. In my experience, there's no better way to gain confidence than by practicing your skills. You practice your skills by doing the activities, and you commit to the high-impact activities by engaging your Rainmaker's Achievement Cycle. This places you in the highest theater of learning: trial and error. Through trial, error, and effort, Rainmakers master the key skills needed for high-impact prospecting activities.

Finessing Introductions & Referrals

How do you get introductions and referrals from affluent clients and strong centers-of-influence? Simple: you ask for them—but in a subtle way. Obviously, your goal is getting face-to-face with a new prospect. And unless your client or center-of-influence is an idiot (and I'm sure that isn't the case), he's well aware of your strategic intent. Still, it's important that your request for an introduction be framed as a "meet and greet," not a sales pitch session. This is one of the activities that appears simple at first glance, but requires a high degree of skill. I'll illustrate the difference in the following dialogue, which I call "Disco Salesman vs. the Seamless Seller." (The old-fashioned referrals approach was favored by 1970s insurance salesmen—hence, the word "disco.")

DISCO SALESMAN: "[NAME], I really appreciate you as a client, and I hope you can see the value in all the work that I've done for you and your family. We make our living by working with good people like you, [NAME], and we really appreciate your business. We build our business through the referrals we get from good clients like you. That way, I can focus more on serving our clients. So, [NAME], we make a point of meeting periodically with our better clients in order to ask for three to five referrals."

That's the old-fashioned approach to referrals. In some instances, Disco Salesman would ask you to immediately go to your rolodex, and write down the contact information of three to five referrals. Or, he'd simply hand you some business cards and ask that you give them to people he believes would benefit from his services. As you recall some of the other techniques from yesteryear, you'll probably cringe. Do you remember the one where you placed "Referrals" at the top of a sheet of paper with 10 to 20 blanks lines, so your client could fill in contact names? And of course, there was the passive referral request that appeared at the bottom of some nonsense letter you sent. The list goes on, but you get the idea. Sure, these are activities. But they don't possess the finesse necessary for today's affluent world. In fact, requesting referrals in such a way is not just ineffective, but it tends to cheapen the professionalism of the person asking. No one should be begging for business. However, every Rainmaker makes his living by skillfully obtaining high-quality introductions and referrals.

Meanwhile, the Seamless Seller already has a good relationship with his client. He knows the client works with Bob, plays golf with Joe, and runs half-marathons with Mary. The Seamless Seller also knows that golfing buddy Bob has lots of money, and that he's an attorney. So the Seamless Seller carefully picks an optimum moment.

SEAMLESS SELLER: "Say, you know your golfing buddy, Bob—the attorney? I'd really like to play golf with him some day. In fact, let's all play golf, my treat . . ."

Is that simple? Yes.

Is it easy? Not always. If it was, everyone would be doing it.

The Seamless Seller asks directly for the introduction, but packages it in a non-threatening way. As a Rainmaker, the Seamless Seller understands that less is better—less verbiage, less foreplay, less dancing around the issue of getting face-to-face. They have mastered the skill of being both subtle and direct.

You don't play golf? Then invite your client to bring Bob to a ball game. Or invite everyone out for drinks or coffee or sushi—it doesn't matter. What matters is that your chosen activity (and the venue) is safe and non-threatening. That way, the invitee won't worry that you'll corner him with a high-pressure sales spiel for 60 minutes.

SEAMLESS SELLER: "Oh by the way, if Bob asks about our relationship, just say I'm the person who oversees and coordinates your financial affairs—or your family's financial affairs (or your legal affairs/ family's legal affairs, etc.)."

Why add this last sentence? Because the Seamless Seller doesn't want Bob pigeonholing him as some eager salesman on the prowl. The Seamless Seller is always subtle, but never too subtle. For example, he might also say, "Don't hesitate to sing my praises if Bob asks, but you don't need to go into details about my business." This is a Rainmaker at his best; subtle but direct, with everything linked to his objective.

Be Yourself . . . At Your Best

It all begins with refining your image. Your personality, your image, your first impression are all extremely important. A true Rainmaker pays careful attention to his grooming and dress. He doesn't try to overdress, but he *never* under-dresses. (When in doubt, the Rainmaker plays it safe by dressing a half-notch up.)

In addition, Rainmakers understand fundamental social graces. One of my women clients even attended a finishing school to boost her confidence in this area. For her, it wasn't really a matter of distinguishing between the various spoons and forks at formal dinner parties, but of learning the ABCs of formal dress and etiquette—just in case. She even went as far as practicing in front of a mirror and visualizing each encounter. More than anything else, this served to build her confidence so she could apply the Rainmaking skills she was learning.

I've known other people who've taken courses in diction and accent elimination. Personally, I don't think it's necessary to erase your Brooklyn accent. But if it makes you more comfortable, feel free to hire a modern-day Henry Higgins. You probably don't need an extreme makeover—just fitted suits and a stylish haircut.

A Rainmaker may or may not look like James Bond (or one of the Bond girls), but he or she knows how to behave at a baseball game—how to eat a hot dog and spill mustard on his/her pants just like the rest of us. And the Rainmaker also knows how to eat in the finest restaurant or country club in the land. Seriously, unless you were raised by werewolves, you probably don't need to attend finishing school.

On the other hand, it couldn't hurt to consult resources such as the following:

- John T. Malloy's dress for success.
- Dale Carnegie for confidence.
- Toastmasters for public speaking
- www.emilypost.com for etiquette

Even more important than etiquette is the ability to shift gears. You really have to know yourself. You don't need to be the most mannerly person, but you don't wipe your nose on your sleeve either. Just be comfortable in your own skin, and understand the rules of engagement for a variety of different situations.

Social self-consciousness is your worst enemy. It's amazing how many people are intimidated by status. They walk into that fancy restaurant, and they're too self-conscious to be themselves. You don't have to be perfectly aligned to all of the little idiosyncrasies of the country club or whatever, but you have to be confident that you won't make a fool of yourself. It's simple, but requires confidence. Don't be someone you're not.

Common Nonsense

Most people violate the rules of engagement because they try too hard. Their insecurity forces them to try to dominate the conversation. They feel as though it's "SHOW TIME," and engage in a wide range of rude and inappropriate behavior.

They talk too much and too loudly.

They tell inappropriate jokes.

They order the most expensive bottle of wine, and get sloppy drunk.

They talk religion.

They talk politics.

They tell sexual jokes or make sexual advances.

They do all of the above after getting sloppy drunk.

For the shy and reticent, the temptation to grease the wheels with a little booze can be especially tempting, but it often leads to embarrassment. Years ago, a friend invited a group of affluent backers to the Dramatists Guild in New York City to watch a staged reading of his latest Off-Broadway comedy. Having spent thousands of dollars to rent the space, hire actors, stage the event, and provide wine and cheese for the after-theater soiree, the playwright proceeded to make an ass of himself.

During the performance, he became so nervous that he drank buckets of merlot, and could barely stand by the end of the night. At the party, as potential financiers surrounded him with their congratulations, he alternately insulted and ignored them. He even asked one business owner why he was wearing SCUBA gear. (The man was actually wearing a green turtleneck.)

Let's be careful out there, people.

You may be a funny person, but you don't want to tell the wrong joke. Not everybody with money is a Republican. You don't want to tell racial jokes, ethnic jokes, minority jokes, sex jokes—unless (maybe) you're in a locker room somewhere and somebody's told you one. But, be very careful. I've seen people get themselves into real trouble telling jokes, by being sloppy with alcohol or by being too opinionated and getting into a political or intellectual argument.

Rainmakers are skilled communicators. They can discuss a variety of subjects on a variety of levels. They can talk with you about recent books, changes in the tax codes, what they think about steroids in baseball, or the FEMA response to Hurricane Katrina –without introducing controversy. Yes, they're good communicators, but they also respect certain boundaries. They follow the old adage about avoiding three topics in polite society—politics, religion and sex.

Many salespeople put down the competition, but this is sheer stupidity. It often starts when the prospect complains about an investment vehicle or the firm that recommended it. "I bought this other fund from a financial advisor, and it tanked." Now, you jump in, and trash it too. This is like insulting somebody's mother just because the daughter spent the last half-hour whining about her. The daughter can do it, but you must not.

If the prospect expresses dissatisfaction, quickly suggest ways to extricate her from that situation—without bashing the competition. If you bash the competition, and especially if you jump on board and start poking fun, you're basically calling the prospect a dope for having hired the firm and purchased that product or service.

Create a Warm Sales Environment

Beyond working on your interpersonal skills, you need to create a sales environment that is warm, friendly and inviting—an environment that serves as an extension of your personality and professional image. And that includes the appearance and perceived attitude of any staff members making the first contact with prospects as they arrive in your office. (Sullen, gum-snapping receptionists are fine for Russian government offices, but not for a business that needs to generate profits.)

While driving through a small town, have you ever passed the offices of an insurance firm or realtor (I'm not naming any names) that looks like it was last painted when cars came standard-equipped with V-8 engines and tailfins? I have, and I've never been temped to enquire within. Don't let this be your office.

Your sales environment doesn't have to look like a Las Vegas casino—or Donald Trump's boardroom—but it needs to project warmth, friendliness and service-orientation. This is where many securities firms and banks fail. As the customer, you arrive to a sterile lobby, with a glum receptionist behind a desk. Then you wait . . . and wait . . . with nothing but a pile of year-old magazines for company.

A Rainmaker wouldn't keep you there for more than 30 seconds. And when he arrived, he'd greet you with your choice of coffee and 16 flavors of bagels, croissants, muffins and Danish.

I visit scores of financial service firms, and many of the offices are quite nice—on the outside. In any major city today, it's especially important to project a warm and friendly environment, because prospects now have to pass through so many layers of security, thanks to 9/11. It's not very warm and friendly, so the environment within your office needs to be. If your reception area has room for just a few chairs, make sure the magazines are current; make certain that you good have a good relationship with the receptionist; make certain that the receptionist knows whom you're expecting. Be sure that you or your assistant (preferably you) go out to greet that client as soon as he/she arrives. Even if the place looks nice, you don't want people waiting for 15 minutes or more.

A Word on Feedback

Client satisfaction surveys are very much in vogue these days. My advice: Don't *ever* distribute one of these to an affluent client!

A true Rainmaker is a high-level relationship manager with his finger on the pulses of his best relationships. He never—*ever*—insults his best clients by sending out satisfaction surveys. The Rainmaker continually interacts with his clients on a personal level, and quickly learns what he could be doing better. He doesn't need to ask, "Hey, what could we be doing better?" He already knows the answer, and he's already taken corrective action, if necessary.

Remember, affluent clients have to like you, trust you, and respect you as a professional. When one of these client satisfaction surveys arrives from the home office, the first thing your client does is throw it away. Secondly, they ask you, "Why the hell did they send me this thing? You're doing a great job. I don't have time to fill out a five-page form."

If I take my Mercedes, BMW or Affinity to the dealership for servicing, and a week later, I receive a satisfaction survey on how everything went, my reaction is, "Give me a break." On the other hand, if my car is returned—hand-washed and detailed (with even the wheels cleaned), with a personal note from the service manager—then I won't mind receiving a call from dealership asking me if everything was OK. That's not an annoyance. That's strong. That's personal. They've given me a little extra value, and proven they really care.

Ask, Listen and *Then* Respond

A vital Rainmaker skill is the ability to ask good questions. Questions can do more to establish your competence than any statement. Questions draw out valuable information and opinions that you can use to personalize your response and whatever you are planning to present. Questions convince people that you're truly interested in them—their needs, ideas, opinions and feelings.

You must also become a good listener. That means really listen! Don't start thinking about your response, or you will miss something important. Take notes, when appropriate. Ask for further clarification. Nod your head and give short acknowledgements such as, "That's great," "You must have been proud of that," "That's helpful to know."

Practice incorporating what you've heard into your responses, and into anything you present later. Use such phrases such as, "You mentioned that . . . ", "Since you stated that _____ is important to you . . ." or "You asked about . . ."

Good questions are truly great persuaders and relationship builders. Remember, everything about a Rainmaker involves relationships.

No man ever listened himself out of a job.
— Calvin Coolidge, 30th President of the United States

SUMMARY

Rainmaking skills are *interpersonal skills* that envelope high-level sales skills. This mastery requires a blend of common sense, courtesy and finely tuned antennae. The Rainmaker refines her selling skills by performing the right activities. In the beginning, you may not be confident or comfortable doing what it takes. But waiting to feel comfortable won't solve anything. You want to feel the fear and act in the face of it.

Often the difference between and a Rainmaker and a wannabe is the skill of getting high-quality introductions and referrals. This is one of those, "What came first, the chicken or the egg?" issues. And the solution is common sense. You will improve your introduction- and referral-generation skills through action. It's no coincidence that Rainmakers consistently engage in high-impact prospecting activities and are constantly working on their skills. Activities and skills go hand-in-hand.

This leads to dressing the part. Many people consider this an art, and I wouldn't argue the point. But I view it as a skill, because the key is learning to become comfortable in your own skin. Naturally, you need to avoid the kind of "common nonsense" that afflicts the insecure, especially the temptation to "grease the wheels" with alcohol.

As a Rainmaker, you should know your clients well enough to avoid developing (or even forwarding) client satisfaction surveys. Also remember to create a warm and inviting sales environment to show prospects that you really care about their comfort and the first impression you make. Finally, force yourself to ask, listen and *then* respond.

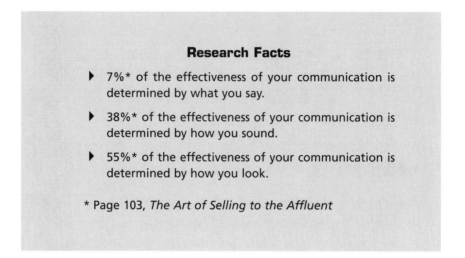

Research Facts

▶ 7%* of the effectiveness of your communication is determined by what you say.

▶ 38%* of the effectiveness of your communication is determined by how you sound.

▶ 55%* of the effectiveness of your communication is determined by how you look.

* Page 103, *The Art of Selling to the Affluent*

TAKING ACTION

- Check out some of the recommended reading listed in this chapter.
- Review your Top 25 client inventory, and identify 10 clients and two centers-of-influence who you will contact to get an introduction.
- Do your homework with these clients and centers-of-influence so that you have a specific name or two for them to introduce you to.
- Practice your subtle but direct approach in front of a mirror.
- Have one face-to-face each working day to engage in this introduction-generating activity and work on your skills.
- If you were to design a client satisfaction survey, which questions would you ask? Now, without ever creating a written survey, listen for the answers whenever you meet with your best clients.

10

Use the Web (Your Prospects Do)

The affluent use the Internet extensively for research.
—Factoid, 2004 APD Research

The Internet has more to offer than the opportunity to duplicate your identity in cyberspace. Because it offers the fastest and most effective access to information, it can make a huge difference in your Rainmaking efforts. It's a Rainmaker's dream regarding intel.

Common Sense Revisited

In Chapter 5, you were introduced to the high-impact prospecting activities related to targeted networking, introductions, and referrals. The emphasis in each activity is on building relationships—to create emotional equity with the movers and shakers you want to attract as clients. The Internet can play a vital role in helping you discover valuable and timely facts about those movers and shakers.

Begin with the name of an individual from your *Top 25 Introduction Notebook* (see page 63)—someone you want to meet so you can begin the relationship-building process. The more you know about them, the easier it will be for you to ask questions and ultimately find something in common. Here's the drill.

Go to Google.com, and enter the individual's full name followed by his/her city and state. Example: Matt Oechsli Greensboro NC. The listings that result when you click the SEARCH button will include news items about the individual, websites where his/her name appears, quotes made by others about them, and any other item from Google's database in which the individual's name appears. Next, look at the links above the box at the top where you entered the name. At this point, you've been looking at information about the individual on the *Web*. You should also explore the following . . .

- *Images*—You may discover a photo of the individual from a news story or some other source.
- *News*—You can read the latest news items on the individual. And, by clicking on "News Alerts" on your left, you can sign up to have news items about this individual sent to you via e-mail—at no cost. This gives you an opportunity to send "I noticed in the news . . ." notes on the very day the item appears.
- *Web*—Return to the Web link, and enter the individual's home phone number (e.g., 336-273-6582). At the top of the page, you'll see "Phone book results for (phone number)." It will provide you with the address—and with links to Google Maps, Yahoo Maps and Map Quest. Click on Google Maps and notice how clearly you can identify the neighborhood in which she lives. How close is it to you? What's the income level of people in that area? What does her residence's location tell you about her? Then look at the other listing on that page. You may discover information that did not appear in your initial search. If you want to know about the location of her business, enter her business phone number.

You need to be careful in using this newly gathered intel with affluent prospects. They spook easily, and you don't want them to feel that you violated their privacy or that you're stalking them. However, if you know that someone started his business in 1987, graduated from Yale law school, played minor league baseball, plays the violin in the local orchestra, or is actively involved in a particular charity, these are safe places to start your rapport building. The idea is to let your successful prospect talk about his successes and interests.

Also, I must warn you of the black hole of cyberspace. Get your intel and get out. More people waste time on the Internet than anywhere else that I know.

Your Place In Cyberspace

Although the affluent rely heavily on the opinions of trusted friends and associates to recommend particular service providers, the vetting process doesn't stop there. Avid Internet users, affluent consumers often conduct extensive online searches for the best mix of products, services, features, options and fees. If you haven't launched your own website yet, consider doing so *very* soon. But don't put up a site just because it seems fashionable, or because many of your competitors are doing so. Either do it right, or don't do it at all.

Many of the world's 36 million websites are resting peacefully in the Internet graveyard. They are nothing more than online billboards, brochures or catalogs that feature lists of products, value propositions and testimonials. They are rarely visited, and if they are, most visitors will leave after about 10 seconds, never to return. Your site needs to offer more than that. The purpose of having a website is to pull targeted visitors toward the point of sale. As high-end service providers, it's doubtful you'll make any sales based solely on your site's copy and design, but you can go a long way toward helping affluent prospects clearly understand who you are, what you offer, and why you are superior to your rivals.

To attract affluent visitors, you must ensure that your site is easy to find, and easy to navigate. Your site must offer compelling reasons to fully explore your positioning, prices, products and services. Everything—absolutely everything—begins with selecting the right keywords and phrases. These keywords and phrases help you:

- Define your unique Internet niche and describe your business to others.
- Describe what you offer in terms of how your products and services provide value and solutions for your clients.

- Create a logo and tag line that immediately convince visitors that they've come to the right place.
- Help you decide how to organize your site so that targeted visitors can easily determine where they want to go next.
- Create titles, headings and content that relates to the interests and needs of targeted visitors.

Most important, you must choose appropriate keywords and phrases to help potential visitors actually find your site, and find it quickly—before they decide to browse your competitors' sites instead. If you've ever searched for a product or service provider in your region—from plumbers and house painters to accountants and attorneys—you know that search results often turn up hundreds, and even thousands, of pages listing related websites. And if you're like the vast majority of Web surfers, you'll only browse through the first page or so of the results to find what you want, leaving the sites on subsequent pages to languish in obscurity.

What does it take to be listed on the first page of a search engine like Google? To answer these questions, it's important to have a basic understanding of how information is organized, classified and presented on the Internet.

Search Engines and Directories

Search engines like Google, and directories such as Yahoo, base everything on keywords and phrases. If someone is looking for a financial advisor, they will enter "financial advisor" in the box provided, and then click on the SEARCH button. As a result, they will see a list of 10 to 12 websites that include "financial advisor" in the list of keyword phrases the website owners used when submitting their website to be listed in that search engine or directory. Actually, the listings are for single web pages, not entire websites.

Both search engines and directories use what are called "relevancy" factors to determine which websites to accept for listing. Search engines use software to "read" webpage content, check links, and calculate relevancy. Directories rely on the information submitted, and that information is typically evaluated by human reviewers who actually visit the website. Search engines index websites by keyword. Directories index sites under categories, and then by keyword. However, there is little distinction today between how people use search engines vs. directories. If you go to Google (search engine) or Yahoo (directory), you'll begin your search by entering a keyword or phrase in the box and clicking on the SEARCH button.

Tips and Tools

If you have a website and want people to find it, you will want to be listed in the top 10 search engines and directories. But don't try to submit your website yourself. There are too many factors that need your attention, and it will require considerable research on your part to learn all that. Instead, find someone in your area who's an expert in submitting websites to search engines and directories, and pay them to assist you. They will help you select keyword phrases and optimize your website to significantly increase the probability that you will be listed. They will then submit your key web pages to the top 10 search engines and directories, carefully following the specific requirements for each one.

Another option is paying to have your website listed, and you can do that yourself with Google, which is one of the most popular search engines. Go to www.google.com. Then click on the "Advertising Programs" link. There you will find the link to "Google AdWords." Click on that link, and the world of pay-per-click Internet advertising will be opened unto you. Google does an excellent job in guiding you through the sign-up process. Activating an account only costs $5.00. They provide clear instructions and lots of tips on doing it right. As you are setting up your website to be listed—which will appear on the right side of the page under your selected keyword phrase—you will also learn a lot about the world of Internet advertising.

Do's and Don'ts of Design

If I were to build a website specifically designed to *repel* affluent buyers, I'd cram it with unnecessary graphics, gismos and banners scrolling from left to right, up and down or diagonally. It would resemble Times Square on New Year's Eve—noisy, confusing and cluttered. You'd get a headache looking at it.

Of course, some people take the opposite tack—designing sites so Spartan they can truly be described as minimalist. The managing partner of one Wall Street law firm paid a designer to create a graphic-less site in black & white, which featured nothing but a few paragraphs about the company and its partners, as well as a list of his favorite restaurants. What was the point of that?

By contrast, a Rainmaker's site is always understated and professional, with no glitz and no marquees. When a visitor arrives, it should take them only 10 seconds to know that they've arrived at the right website, and another 10 seconds to decide where to go next. *That* is the key first factor in pulling them toward the point of sale—your site must provide clear navigation instructions, making it easy enough for a toddler to find her way.

Everything is clear, clean and functional. Your visitors know exactly where they are at all times, and they know exactly who you are and what you do. This means that your copy is simple and communicates clearly. How does someone check out XYZ service? Double click on this link. What if I have a question? Press there, or call this number. FYI: it's important to make a real human being available to answer prospects' questions or fulfill requests for information. Your e-mail address or phone number should appear on every page.

Like your physical sales environment, your website should project warmth and friendliness, and display a personal touch. Most important, *update your site on a regular basis!* If you're not going to invest in keeping your site updated, you're better off not launching one. You'll look outdated after only a few months. Unfortunately, some service providers decide to construct sites on the cheap, and don't maintain them. Don't you do that!

Hiring Designers and Copywriters

Unless you're a very talented do-it-yourselfer with plenty of spare time (and Rainmakers never have much spare time), you'll need to outsource the design, copywriting and launch of your website. When deciding which web designer and/or copywriter to hire, take the same approach to the hiring process that affluent consumers take regarding major purchase decisions. Consult with colleagues, friends, family, friends of friends, and others you trust for referrals to skilled professionals. In addition, you might check out various outsourcing websites such as www.elance.com and www.guru.com to locate the right people.

As a prospective buyer, you can subscribe to these sites free of charge, and then post your project for competitive bidding. In your posting, outline your project parameters, budget range, deadline expectations and other specifications. As freelancers bid for the contract, be sure to examine their online resumes and/or profiles listed at the site, as well as their portfolios. If the designer or writer hasn't uploaded a portfolio, ask to see samples of his or her work. Since most of these sites let past clients rate their experiences and post feedback comments, be sure to check these out, too. Many freelancers also list references, but there's nothing like unsolicited and unbiased feedback to separate the hacks from the pros. Even if a friend or colleague referred the person, it's still important to conduct a background check. Call other people who've used them in the past to make sure they produce high-quality sites on a consistent basis. Whether you take the online or offline route, it's also a good idea to give the designer some examples of sites that you'd like him or her to use as models.

By the way, there are individuals who will offer to design your site *and* write the copy, but I'd be skeptical about hiring someone to provide both of these services. Although websites blend computer graphics design and ad copywriting, it's rare to find a single individual who displays adequate talent in both fields. It's a bit like hiring an architect to design your house *and* construct the furniture. Yes, there *are* people who can do this, but not very many.

Choose your freelancers carefully, and lend as much support and direction as necessary. If your team is any good, they should be able to answer almost any question you throw their way. They'll know which fonts and point sizes are easiest to read, how colors influence visitor behavior, and how to select an appropriate navigation system. They should also be able to help you in selecting the best keywords and phrases to employ. But don't take their word for everything. Use your own tastes and preferences to help guide your decisions, and "beta test" your site with friends and colleagues before your launch.

Keep in mind that your website projects your Internet image. It is your brand. It helps you position vis-à-vis the competition. By itself, your site won't make you a Rainmaker. It's an ancillary tool. But it can be an invaluable supplement for assisting the affluent in making their purchase decisions.

SUMMARY

There is a lot of information on the Internet about the affluent people you want to attract as new clients. Enter their names and locations in Google.com, and go from there.

Affluent consumers conduct extensive online searches to find the best mix of products, services, features, options and fees. If you haven't launched a website yet, consider doing so *very* soon. But do the job right, or don't do it all—and that includes spending time and money to update your site on a regular basis. In tandem with your web designer and copywriter, select keywords and phrases to define your company, its products and services, and the advantages of purchasing from you. Links to helpful online resources will not only help prospects make their purchase decisions, they can make it easier to find your website when searching with Internet directories and search engines.

Outsource the design and copywriting of your site to the best professionals you can locate. Check out their backgrounds and previous work, and feel free to solicit their advice when choosing specific features for your site. Your website not only projects your online image, it can also help persuade prospects to choose you over your competitors.

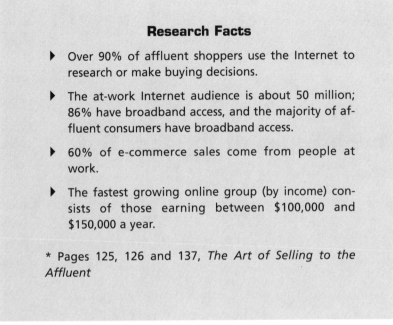

Research Facts

▶ Over 90% of affluent shoppers use the Internet to research or make buying decisions.

▶ The at-work Internet audience is about 50 million; 86% have broadband access, and the majority of affluent consumers have broadband access.

▶ 60% of e-commerce sales come from people at work.

▶ The fastest growing online group (by income) consists of those earning between $100,000 and $150,000 a year.

* Pages 125, 126 and 137, *The Art of Selling to the Affluent*

TAKING ACTION

- Search through Google.com to find valuable information on 5 select affluent prospects from your Top 25 Introduction Notebook.
- Use that information to create appropriate questions to ask when you are face-to-face with each prospect, and also note anything you have in common.
- Be careful of the information you use, since affluent prospects spook easily.
- If you haven't yet launched a website, get started. Contact web designers and copywriters to learn about prices, features and options. Also, visit your competitors' websites to determine what works and what doesn't.
- If you have an existing site, when was the last time it was updated? Visit yourself online to determine if anything could, or should, be modified.

11

Psych Yourself Up, Not Out

> "A journey of a thousand miles must begin with a single step."
>
> —Lao Tsu

I was on an airplane when I met Rick, the "gun-to-the-head" Rain-maker whose story I shared with you in Chapter 4. As I mentioned, he was a young man when he began working at one of the "Big 4" accounting firms. He'd been hired after graduating from Duke and then passing his CPA exam. Just out of school, he went for his first job interview, and was hired to be a Rainmaker. Seconds after shaking his hand, Rick's new boss gave him a folder. "Kid, you've got a year to bring in 15 companies from that folder as clients. If you do that, you'll have a chance at a career here. Good luck."

Let me share a little more light on Rick's initial foray into his craft. "I mean, first I was happy to get the job," said Rick. "And then I realized, 'Holy crap! He's asking me to *sell!* I don't know how to sell. I'm a CPA.'" Since quitting was not an option, Rick concentrated on how to identify at least one key person per company. Then he identified just one individual at one company, and started following him—almost like a stalker.

"I found out that this guy would eat breakfast at this one diner every morning, and he'd eat with the same two or three guys. So I started eating breakfast at the same diner. After two weeks of this, I was so frustrated with not knowing what to do that I bumped into him and knocked over his breakfast tray. I bought him breakfast, and ultimately his company became my first client."

"Not knowing what else to do, I continued that same strategy for the rest of the year. By the time I went for my performance review, I was convinced I'd be fired because I'd only brought in 12 new relationships. Well, I wasn't fired. Instead, the boss doubled my compensation, and said, 'Now if you want to get your comp doubled next year, you'd better bring in 15 new clients.'

"I laughed, and then it hit me: I'd just become a Rainmaker."

Most of us are not strangers to the kind of pressures faced by Rick. Thankfully, Rick was able to successfully translate the pressure into the kind of energy needed to pursue the right Rainmaking activities. Although he didn't know it at the time, he began developing the mindset of a Rainmaker by activating the Rainmaker's Achievement Cycle.

Some people aren't as fortunate as Rick, who by his own account, stumbled into activating his Rainmaker's Achievement Cycle. In the financial services and legal professions, where work environments can be truly toxic, too many people succumb to the stress, and become driven by their feelings, turning to drugs, alcohol (and even suicide) for relief. Instead of activating their Rainmaker's Achievement Cycle by committing to a goal and engaging in high-impact activities, they are driven by how they feel. They feel pressure; they feel unsure; they feel unqualified; they feel self-conscious. Regardless of what they feel, listening to these feelings de-activates their Rainmaker's Achievement Cycle. More often than not, this has serious negative repercussions.

According to surveys conducted by the American Bar Association and various state bar associations, lawyers suffer from extremely high rates of substance abuse, depression and suicide. I don't have any statistics for the financial services industry, but I'm sure the figures are comparable.

Remember Peter, the Rainmaker introduced in Chapter 1? Peter once told me, "I'm going to become a Rainmaker if it kills me." He was speaking metaphorically, of course, but that may not be true of everyone reading this book. If you're suffering from any of the problems described above, please set down this book and seek professional help.

You might also want to consider getting into another profession. It's not worth risking your health or your very life to pursue objectives that are killing you in the process. There are other ways to achieve prosperity *and* peace of mind.

Assuming you're healthy and mentally sound, there are three things you can do to stay that way, and become a better Rainmaker en route.

1. **Raise and maintain your energy level:** "To be a rainmaker, you need a phenomenal amount of energy," says Peter. "I'm spending 70% of my time with my wealthiest clients, their centers-of-influence, my centers-of-influence or wealthy prospects. I've got to be on my A-Game, and that takes a tremendous amount of energy."

   Peter's regimen is something we should all follow. First of all, he stays in shape. You don't necessarily have to join a gym or start running marathons. Take short walks on your lunch hour, whenever possible, or after work. Sign up for the company softball team, or play some golf or tennis on the weekends. Have fun while you exercise. I don't mean to sound clichéd, but it *is* important to get your sleep, work out and exercise, and eat properly. This doesn't mean you can't drink alcohol, and it doesn't mean you can't enjoy ice cream and chocolate mousse. Just be aware of how your lifestyle impacts your energy levels, and do what it takes to stay fit.

   We've found that when people are aware of their energy levels, they have more energy, because they're careful with their bodies. A Rainmaker realizes that his/her body is the temple. You can't be making rain if you've got a headache, or if you chain-smoke to the point where you can barely breathe. Rarely will you find a Rainmaker who's a hypochondriac. Rarely will you find a Rainmaker who isn't in good health. So get yourself in shape. Rainmaking is not for the weak and weary.

   Being in shape will also help you cope with stress. In fact, as you probably know, exercise can be a wonderful antidote for stress. A Rainmaker knows how to handle stress, and never internalizes it. He finds ways of releasing stress. Personally, I prefer yoga, and I always eat right—even when I'm on the road. I'll have a glass or two of wine with dinner, but I don't drink the whole bottle.

2. **Stay Focused:** "Each time I come into the office," says Peter, "there are at least 10 legitimate items that can pull me off track: problems, issues, must-dos. I need to dot the i's, cross the t's, work with support staff, and then get out of Dodge to do my Rainmaking activities. I can't get bogged down. It requires the discipline of focus—extraordinary focus."

Easier said than done, right? Yes, but there are any number of time savers that you can effectively employ to help you focus on your Rainmaking activities while still accomplishing your other tasks and responsibilities. Here's a short list of time-saving tips compiled by Paul Lemberg, President of Quantum Growth Coaching, Inc.

- **Minimize Time Spent in Meetings.** Meetings often squander huge amounts of time—and not just yours. Some meetings are called simply for the convenience of the caller, without regard to anyone else's time constraints. Just say no! It's up to you to maximize what you get done during a day, week or year. Believe me when I say, no one else cares about your time. This means you must choose which meetings to attend and which to politely decline. Depending on your position, this single act could save you 10 to 20 hours a week, or more. This may be hard for many of you, especially if your company supports open communication and lots of meetings. Still, ask yourself whether your attendance will make a greater or lesser contribution to the company than the Rainmaking activities on your agenda. If *you've* called the meeting, stay on track. Stick to the agenda, and don't let anyone hijack your meeting.
- **Schedule Times for Answering Phone Calls.** Before you

place calls, identify and develop a desired outcome for each call. Then make certain you achieve that outcome. Unscheduled, inbound calls are a big time waster, but you have a few options:

- *Don't answer your phone.* Let voicemail do it, and return only those calls that are important.
- *Answer calls only during certain hours,* and let everyone know those hours. You can even put that notice on your voicemail message. "If you want to reach me live, call between…" Alternatively, you could specify a time during which you will return calls.
- *When you're involved with focused work—such as writing or thinking—don't answer the phone.* Better yet, put it on "do not disturb," so it doesn't even ring. Also, tell friends and family not to call you at work except during certain hours or—obviously—in case of emergencies.
- When you answer a call from someone other than a client or prospect, keep schmoozing to a minimum, and ask the caller his purpose. It isn't impolite. In fact, many people find it refreshing when you ask, "Why are you calling?" Finally, have a clock facing you while you're on the phone. This will remind you of the time. Of course, none of this suggests that if you do valuable business on the phone, you should stop doing it. Just be conscious of the time being spent.

- **Treat E-Mail Like the Phone.** E-mail has become another great sink-hole of time. I'm a huge fan of e-mail. It's one of the greatest communications media of our time. But it can really eat into your schedule. So, treat e-mail like the phone. Shut down your e-mail programs, and open them only when you're ready. Limit your mail checking to specific times of day, and delete *anything* that's not relevant.

Use the subject headers as a guide, and don't even bother to read the message if the subject isn't for you.

- **Drop-ins.** Many managers cultivate an open door policy. While this is very warm and egalitarian, it can also use up copious amounts of time. What to do? For one, you can open your door on a schedule. Maintain an open door—if you must—only during certain hours. That limits interruptions to a specific period. When someone comes in, politely ask him to get to the point. "How can I help you?" or "What do you need from me?" or "What do you want to achieve?" And so on. After you've run this drill for a while, time-wasters will get the idea, and start bothering someone else. If you manage a staff, we recommend you schedule weekly meetings with each staff member. You'll cover all your routine matters during that period and use the surplus time for deepening your relationships—even for developmental thinking. This also cuts down on the need for ad-hoc meetings.

- **Plan Your Day.** Develop a prioritized "to-do" list every day, and limit the list to just seven items. You'll rarely accomplish all seven tasks, but if you're a genuine "wunderkind," try listing nine items. But go no farther than nine. I suggest you write your list as the last scheduled activity of each day. Why? Closure. It puts a period on the day, and purges your mind of whatever's on your schedule for tomorrow. If you wait until the next morning, you'll have to carry around your "to-do" list in your head until then. What a waste of personal time!

3. **Be Persistent, But Not a Pain in the Neck:** The affluent make decisions on their own timeline, not yours. Peter once had lunch with an affluent prospect, and within 10 minutes of the lunch conversation, he was told, "I really like your style. I've been looking for someone like you. You're going to be my guy." On another occasion, Peter met with a prospect over lunch, who said, "I really enjoyed lunch, and I'm very interested in what you

do. Let's pick up this conversation when I come back from my two-month vacation in Europe."

This is why you have to manage your pipeline. A Rainmaker is persistent, and is always managing his pipeline. Some prospects take 10 minutes—but that was a lucky shot—and some might take two weeks. Others might take three months, and some might take years. Be persistent by suggesting a date for a follow-up conversation—whether it's by phone, over lunch or on a weekend fishing trip. But don't overdo the wooing, since all that's likely to accomplish is to annoy the prospective client.

Once in a while, it will become obvious that a prospect is stringing you along, and isn't about to make a purchase during this century. In those cases, you have only one real choice. After recapping the highlights of all your previous conversations, politely force the issue. Ask the person if/when he's ready to do business. If he continues to stall, then discontinue regular communications until the person is ready to play ball. You have other fish to fry.

SUMMARY

Becoming a Rainmaker requires a healthy mind and body. To avoid and overcome stress, follow the recommendations contained in this chapter to:

- Raise and maintain your energy level.
- Acquire and maintain your focus. Learn to better manage your time and priorities, and minimize dealings with the people and things that steal focus.
- Be persistent with your best prospects *without* being a pain in the neck.

Research Facts

▶ The affluent (Rainmakers) deal with a lot of stress. More than 75% of all affluent business owners and self-employed professionals work in excess of 60 hours per week. —Factoid, 2004 Affluent Purchasing Decision Research

▶ Rainmaker wannabes do not engage in enough face-to-face high-impact activity.

▶ Rainmakers focus on their goals, while wannabes are reluctant to commit.

TAKING ACTION

- Get a complete physical.
- If you're not exercising, start. You might consider hiring a personal trainer so that you can develop a routine that fits you.
- If you're already exercising, you might also consider working with a personal trainer for a short period of time—just to vary your routine.
- Eat healthy. If you're uncertain, consult with a nutritionist.
- Make certain you are consistently getting enough sleep.
- Maintain a sense of humor. If you don't have one, develop one.

12

The 12 Commandments of Rainmaking

As one of the founders of the Rainmaker Institute, I devote much of my time and attention to developing Rainmakers. My singular purpose in writing this book is to furnish you with a roadmap for becoming a true Rainmaker—a roadmap based on the most current research. I want you to become intimately familiar with Rainmakers, so you know who they are and what sets them apart. I also want to share our 25 years of hands-on experience in developing and working with Rainmakers.

Paying strict attention to each leg of the Rainmaker's stool will enable you to develop into a true Rainmaker. If you're already a Rainmaker, it will help raise your game and become a Master Rainmaker.

From time to time, it might be helpful to remember that you're venturing onto a "road less traveled" for salespeople. Rainmakers are a rare breed—they are professional salespeople who consistently do what the average salesperson either will not or cannot do.

Rainmaker wannabes will skim these chapters, pluck a few gems with which they're comfortable, and apply them whenever they feel like it. This is precisely why most salespeople will be trapped in "Wannabe Purgatory." A true Rainmaker commits to his craft, systematically works through all the material, participates in all the exercises, and carefully fine tunes his game. A true Rainmaker always strives to become a Master Rainmaker, and a Master never stops striving to improve.

The 12 commandments in this chapter have a twofold objective. The first is to provide one last chance for any Rainmaker wannabes who simply skimmed the material and have yet to make a commitment. To these readers, I say, please reflect on your careers and revisit the benefits—to you and your family—of becoming a true Rainmaker. Hopefully, you will make the decision to start over with the serious intention of becoming a Rainmaker.

My second objective is to provide those of you who are already committed to the mastery of this phenomenal craft with a string of reminders—12 common-sense jewels that are short and sweet, but long on meaning.

I'm frequently asked about my commandments. Many people want to know if these are the only commandments. No. Heck, you could probably create your own and improve on what you're about to read. Therefore, please receive these commandments as my current and best attempt to further assist your Rainmaker quest.

Commandment 1:
Pledge the Rainmaker Covenant

After one of his many tournament victories, golfing great Jack Nicklaus was asked what he thought about his competition. Essentially, Nicklaus said that at least 100 professional golfers on the tour had the talent to win any given tournament. However, only about 20 thought they had a chance to win, and only five expected to win. Those five were the players Nicklaus considered his competition.

What Nicklaus was describing was the type of internal oath made deep within heart and soul of every extraordinary achiever. Whether the achievement relates to golf or financial services, consistent winners make a commitment to fully maximize their God-given potential.

You might think this goes without saying, but . . . how many people do you know on the path to maximizing their potential? Chances are, you know few—if any. You probably know *more* than a few people with the talent to become a Master Rainmaker, but who have settled into comfortable lifestyles in the lower tiers of success, where they rationalize their under-achievement. Sadly, these people have never pledged the Rainmaker's Covenant.

The Rainmaker's Covenant

I,_____, commit my heart and soul to reaching my God-given potential as a Master Rainmaker. I will always strive to perform my tasks with the utmost integrity and professionalism. I commit to being a lifetime learner, both of life and of Rainmaking. I will work studiously to maintain the mindset of a Rainmaker. I will strive to maintain the discipline required to perform my high-impact activities. I will continually refine my Rainmaking skills.

I will do all of this while being a loving, caring spouse, parent, family member and an active contributor to society. To this end, I will make certain to enjoy the fruits of my labor with outward humility and deep-seated pride. Lastly, I will always look for opportunities to mentor future Rainmakers.

This pledge can never be overstated or reinforced enough. Becoming a Master Rainmaker requires total commitment. It cannot be done in a casual manner. Nor can it be accomplished on a part-time basis. You might have the talent, but without this pledge, you will not consistently perform high-impact Rainmaker activities.

This pledge represents a contract with yourself regarding your talent and career. It is essential to believe in both, regardless of what anyone tells you. You can take this to the bank. Most people will not support your efforts to become a Rainmaker. Why? Because you're entering into a world of commitment and achievement they do not understand. Family members and friends are often the worst saboteurs.

Nothing can replace your passion—the can-do mindset you bring to your profession. Don't take this passion for granted. Just because you have it one day is no assurance that it will be there the next. As a Rainmaker, your job is to light this internal fire every day.

Commandment 2: Be Totally Goal Driven

Whether you're like Rick, our "gun to the head" CPA who operated out of fear, or like Peter who personally committed to bringing in "15 new clients this year if it kills me," these goals are what activate the *Rainmaker's Achievement Cycle*. They serve as the focal point, the nucleus, for everything you do. Goals establish direction and create pull. As baseball great turned philosopher Yogi Berra so aptly put it, "If you don't know where you're going, you could wind up someplace else." One of the greatest challenges people face is setting and committing to serious goals. Whether it's because they resist the "gun to the head" or "I'm going to do this if it kills me" mentality, or they simply don't recognize the importance, wannabes rarely activate their achievement cycle. Instead, they stumble through life as chronic underachievers.

The cruel irony is that most people consider themselves to be hard working and goal-oriented when—in harsh reality—they're not. Sure, they've set and achieved goals at various times in the past. But these have been isolated occurrences, not a regular pattern.

There can be no mistake about it—no gray area. Unless you activate your *Rainmaker's Achievement Cycle,* you will never become a Rainmaker. Our students at the Rainmaker Institute are aware during the application process that they must be willing to commit to serious Rainmaker goals. Even then, we frequently find that we must reinforce the issue. Setting serious affluent acquisition targets is where Rainmaking begins. Personally, I'm always pushing people to replicate Rick. I want all of my Rainmaking students to commit to bringing in 15 new affluent relationships over a 12-month horizon. I want that proverbial gun to the head. Without fail, it works!

Commandment 3:
Be Fearless (Mindset of a Warrior)

One of the significant qualities that sets Tiger Woods apart from other professional golfers, according to his swing coach Hank Haney, is that he is fearless. Tiger will make adjustments to his swing, enter a tournament, maybe not perform that well, and then continue to work on his swing. He's not afraid to fail. This is the mindset of a winner, which is why I refer to this quality in two ways: *playing without a net* and the *mindset of a warrior*. Not long ago, someone suggested that I replace the term *warrior* with *pioneer*. OK. Take your pick.

Recently, I had lunch with two successful financial advisors, partners in a wealth management practice. As we discussed their situation, it became apparent that they had all the ingredients to be far more successful. They had the proper structure and process in place, and both were true solutions-providers to their clients. In addition, they were well-known, and traveled in the right circles. But something was missing. As one partner said, "It's like we have this beautiful Ferrari that's always sitting in the garage."

Then, one partner made a comment that spoke volumes, "We have all these good relationships that we've spent years developing, but we don't want to screw them up by trying to sell these people."

Bingo!

The remainder of our discussion revolved around *playing without a net*. They were playing it safe, which is not the style of a Rainmaker. Because they'd been playing it safe, they hadn't been developing their Rainmaking skills. Once I got them to set specific Rainmaker goals, 15 new affluent clients apiece, they understood what activating the *Rainmaker's Achievement Cycle* was about. It meant becoming fearless, regardless of any hesitant thoughts or feelings. It meant learning in the midst of action—of playing without a net.

Commandment 4:
Be Extremely Competitive

Stories of the competitiveness of Michael Jordan, the basketball great who hails from North Carolina, are legendary. As a player at the University of North Carolina Chapel Hill, it's said that Michael would challenge teammates to free-throw shooting contests for a nominal wager (pennies per shot). As an NBA star, Michael was noted for competing as hard, if not harder, in practice than during a game.

Winners are highly competitive. Show me someone who isn't competitive, and I'll show you an under-achiever—not necessarily a loser, but someone who isn't exploiting his or her potential. Show me a salesperson who isn't competitive, and I'll show you a Rainmaker wannabe.

Rainmakers play to win. If a Rainmaker hears about another financial advisor achieving Rainmaker status by bringing in 16 new affluent relationships, he will do everything in his power to bring in 20 new relationships.

Because of this extremely competitive nature, Rainmaker's recognize the importance of staying on top of their games. They play to win—always!

Commandment 5: Be Highly Disciplined

Discipline by itself is a routine. Discipline linked to a strong goal is high-octane fuel for achievement. It takes discipline to activate the *Rainmaker's Achievement Cycle* on a daily basis. On many occasions, you'll feel like blowing off a high-impact activity, but discipline will force you to tow the line.

This high level of discipline speaks to you through your conscience. In the same way that the devilish voice of doubt pulls wannabes off track, the voice of discipline (sometimes manifesting itself as guilt) keeps Rainmakers on track. We all have little voices inside our head. The secret is putting that voice to work for us.

A few years ago, an extremely successful Rainmaker that I'd been coaching was driving me to O'Hare airport. (He was successful to the tune of an annual seven-figure income.) Out of the blue, he asked what set high achievers apart from everyone else in the sales game, since everyone has the same opportunities. After reflecting for a few moments, I answered, "Discipline linked to a goal." My Rainmaker chauffer was quiet for a minute, and then responded, "You're dead on. Every time I achieved a major goal and forgot to set another goal, my discipline slipped."

Discipline linked to a goal is the fuel of every Rainmaker's Achievement Cycle.

Commandment 6: Be Completely Focused

We live in an age of sensory overload, and it's only getting worse. There are so many distractions—so much information bombarding us from every direction—it's increasingly difficult to stay focused. Devices like Blackberry's and smart cell phones, originally designed to make us more productive, have become high-tech distractions. The same is true of the Internet. If you're not completely focused, it's easy to be pulled off the critical Rainmaker path.

In Chapter 9, you learned how to conduct a Google search to acquire background intelligence on a prospect. This is an extremely valuable activity IF you remain focused on only relevant information. Many Rainmakers delegate this information gathering to a support person or an intern. Their focus is on spending 70% of their time face-to-face with qualified affluent prospects, or with those who can introduce or refer them to qualified prospects. Other Rainmakers prefer to do the background work themselves to help strengthen their focus.

As I was writing this chapter, someone called to inquire about our Rainmaker Institute and the coaching involved. He claimed to have all the skills, but simply needed to get refocused. Apparently he'd been building his dream house for the past year, and felt he was only functioning at 65% capacity. "One of the reasons I want to attend the Rainmaker Institute is to regain my focus—and I'm getting excited just thinking about it."

Rainmakers are honest about their strengths and weaknesses, and recognize the importance of staying focused.

Commandment 7: Be Fully Energized

Rainmaking is not for the faint of heart, or for people without strong reserves of energy. The caller I mentioned above exercises every morning at

5:30 a.m., and usually starts his day with a 7 a.m. breakfast meeting. Obviously, he isn't also burning the midnight oil by partying with friends.

This doesn't mean that you need to be a card-carrying health nut or exercise fanatic—not at all. However, it *does* mean that you must conserve your energy and properly allocate it. That is one reason why Rainmakers avoid negative people like the plague. People who constantly complain and focus on problems are an energy drain, and need to be avoided.

Common sense issues such as getting enough sleep, eating properly, exercising consistently, and being careful with alcohol are not always common practice for wannabes. But they are standard operating procedure for Rainmakers.

It's always helpful to have a stress release valve, whether its meditation, yoga, running, listening to music or watching a movie. One of our students recently went through a battery of medical tests attempting to discover why he was losing his concentration and becoming embarrassingly forgetful (he'd forget the background intelligence when he was face-to-face with a prospect). After a month of tests, the diagnosis was stress—too much negative stress. When we tried to analyze what was causing this stress, he admitted that he was trying to do too much outside of work, which caused him to attempt part-time Rainmaking.

As Peter would say, be very covetous of your energy!

Commandment 8: Always Be Persistent

"Nothing in the world can take the place of persistence. Talent will not; nothing is more common than unsuccessful men with talent. Genius will not; unrewarded genius is almost a proverb. Education will not; the world is full of educated derelicts. Persistence and determination alone are omnipotent. The slogan 'Press On' has solved, and always will solve the problems of the human race."

— Calvin Coolidge (1872–1933),
30th president of the United States

Most likely, you can think of many people fitting President Coolidge's descriptions of unfulfilled talent. More often than not, under-achievement is the result of succumbing to the obstacles that life puts in our way. High achievers from all fields work through obstacles. Rainmakers have learned this lesson well.

All Rainmakers know the importance of managing their pipelines. Why? Because they understand that affluent people make decisions on their own time-tables, not theirs. They also recognize that there are a number of potential obstacles which must be overcome before they can transition a prospect into a client.

Many of the obstacles Rainmakers are forced to overcome are in their heads. The biggest obstacle has nothing to do with goals focus, commitment or achievement drive: it's the need for immediate gratification. "I met with Ms. Big. Everything went well and I want her business—NOW." The ability to accept delayed gratification (so you can talk business at the right time) is a critical skill. This was Peter's initial challenge, and the reason he refers to persistence as such an integral part of his success.

"Persistence and determination alone are omnipotent." This could be the Rainmaker creed.

Commandment 9:
Always Have Your Antenna Out

Have you ever noticed that some people always get lucky? You don't really believe in luck, because—like me—you know that everyone makes her own luck. This is true of every Rainmaker I've ever met. They have developed a sixth sense that enables them to detect almost any business opportunity. In other words, their *Rainmaker Antenna* is out at all times.

Whether they're attending a daughter's soccer game, a Christmas party, a bar mitzvah or a board meeting, a true Rainmaker always has her antenna out for any business-related signals. It goes without saying that the Rainmaker, unlike the wannabe, has refined her sales skills to such a degree that she can seamlessly initiate a prospecting move under the right circumstances.

For a true Rainmaker, there is no such thing as refusing to work weekends or discuss business at family events, or feeling self-conscious about making a prospecting move at the country club. Rainmakers love what they do, and are fully aware that some of the best business is done under unusual circumstances. But those circumstances have one thing in common: they are always face-to-face.

In short, Rainmakers are always open for business.

Commandment 10:
Be Seamless In Your Sales Skills

Rule #1 is that the affluent do not like being sold.
Rule #2 reminds us to always remember Rule #1.
Rule #3 takes Rules #1 and #2 with a grain of salt.

In reality, every affluent prospect knows when he or she is being prospected, pitched and closed. You can tack whatever labels you'd like onto the sales process, but the real issue is your level of professionalism. There can be no guesswork for a Rainmaker. Rainmakers anticipate the face-to-face meeting, project an outcome they want to achieve, and work hard to control the process with carefully planned rapport-building questions.

The idea is to refine your sales skills so they are subtle, while remaining assertive and direct. In Chapter 7, I had fun contrasting the Seamless Salesperson to the Disco Salesman. It's important to note how simple the seamless approach truly is. But, do not mistake this simple approach as an "easy" one. Sure, you'll have less verbiage to rehearse, because you'll rely much more on questioning, but you must still rehearse. A Rainmaker diligently practices both the questions and the statements.

It doesn't matter whether you are asking questions, articulating your value, describing what you do, or asking for an introduction. The more you practice, the more natural you will appear, and the better your results will be.

As much as I want you rehearsing, your best classroom is

experiential—the experiences of engaging in high-impact prospecting activities.

Rainmakers constantly practice and execute their skills.

Commandment 11: Be Like Tiger

Now that Michael Jordan is officially retired, let's look to Tiger Woods as the Rainmaker's role model. As I mentioned earlier, Tiger Woods is always striving to improve. He's fearless, and he's the hardest worker on the tour.

No matter how successful you become, re-activate your Rain-maker's Achievement Cycle each and every day. No matter how many times you've asked for, and received, an introduction, work to improve your technique. Regardless of how well you might think you can articulate your value, continue to improve your value proposition. Regardless of how fearless you think you are, look for new ways to expand your comfort zone. And no matter how hard you work, be smart.

Be like Tiger!

Commandment 12: Love the Game

"Sincerity is everything. If you can fake that, you've got it made."
—George Burns

Don't you believe it! You must love what you do in order to excel. Period! Look closely at any high achiever, in any walk of life, and you'll find a person who truly loves what he does. Becoming a true Rain-maker, because of the rewards and challenges involved, epitomizes this "love of the game" theme. There is no other way.

The thrill of the hunt, doing your background intelligence, developing initial rapport, managing your pipeline, seamlessly romancing a prospect into a client, uncovering the next prospect—these are what lights a Rainmaker's fire. The mere thought of engaging in these activities unleashes the endorphin flow that will shift you into high gear.

People know when you love what you do. It's one of those intangibles that always surfaces.

SUMMARY

There is no shortcut to becoming a Rainmaker. Make a habit of periodically reviewing these 12 Commandments and, as every Master Rainmaker, you will find yourself continually improving your game. Be like Tiger!

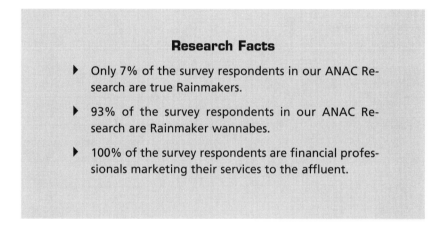

Research Facts

▶ Only 7% of the survey respondents in our ANAC Research are true Rainmakers.

▶ 93% of the survey respondents in our ANAC Research are Rainmaker wannabes.

▶ 100% of the survey respondents are financial professionals marketing their services to the affluent.

TAKING ACTION

- Read Section V carefully.
- Commit to using the *Rainmaker Critical Path System* as outlined in Section V.
- Set firm 12 month Rainmaker goals.
- Act now!

The Rainmaker Critical Path System

Your 12-Month Rainmaker Goal

Now that you know what it takes be become a Rainmaker, you're ready to set your 12-month new affluent client acquisition goal. Remember, your goal is a *statement of intent*. It's what you want, what you will strive for, what you intend to achieve. You have no evidence of what that goal should be and no guarantee of success. What you have is a desire—to match or surpass the "10 or more new affluent clients each year" Rainmaker Standard, or to reach for a number that you believe is realistic for you. This is your first step in developing the fearless mindset of a Rainmaker.

Based on research by David McCelland (Harvard) and John Atkinson (University of Michigan), your greatest goal achievement motivation occurs when you believe you have a 50/50 chance of achieving that goal. With that in mind, it's decision time. Fill in the blank below:

> My GOAL for the next 12 months is to bring in _____
> new Ideal Affluent Clients

Commitment, feedback, support and accountability are the essentials of goal achievement. To make certain you have all of these in place, complete the following:

- I believe I can and will achieve the above goal because:

  _____

- To do so, I must find a way to overcome the following obstacles:

  _____

- The individual who will provide vital feedback, support and accountability to help me stay focused and on task is:

_____

Your Rainmaker Critical Path System

Each week, you engage in a variety of activities related to the personal and business aspects of your life. Because those activities continually compete with each other for your time, it's important to identify and give priority to those *Fixed Daily Activities (FDAs)* that enable you to achieve your goals for attracting new affluent clients, and for retaining and upgrading current clients. These activities are the heart and soul of your Rainmaker Critical Path System.

Defining Rainmaker Critical Path Activities

The Fixed Daily Activities that are critical to your success as a Rainmaker are those high-impact activities I've discussed throughout the text. These are the actions that place you in direct contact with the *people* who will either directly or indirectly build your business:

- Prospects
- Clients
- Internal Advocates
- Referral Alliances Partners
- Important contacts in social, community and industry groups.
- Family members, friends, associates and colleagues who can give qualified introductions and referrals.

As a Rainmaker, your *Critical Path* is defined by the high-impact Fixed Daily Activities you schedule and execute each day to bring new qualified affluent prospects into your pipeline, initiate that first face-to-face meeting with them, follow up to advance the sale, close the sale and clinch the relationship, serve that new client to advance the rela-

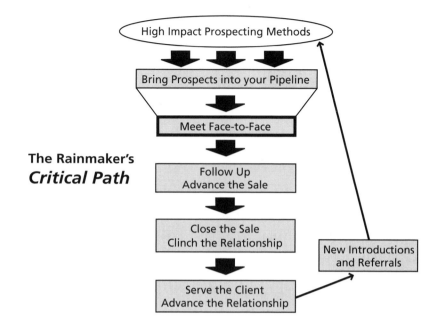

tionship, and then capitalize on the relationship to obtain new introductions and referrals.

To make the above model your reality, you must be engaged each day in the following high-impact Fixed Daily Activities (FDAs):

1. High-impact prospecting FDAs to bring new qualified affluent prospects into your pipeline. They enter your pipeline as a result of your first face-to-face meeting with them. Those FDAs include …

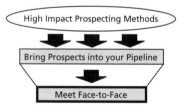

   • Arranging introductions and getting referrals.
   • Networking social, community and industry groups.
   • Build strategic referral alliances.
   • Holding intimate client events.

2. FDAs following the first face-to-face meeting with a qualified affluent prospect to …

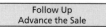

- Build the relationship.
- Establish professional respect.
- Earn trust.

3. FDAs that will enable you to . . .

| Close the Sale |
| Clinch the Relationship |

- Identify verbal and visual buying signals.
- Use the right approach to close the sale.
- Successfully respond to objections or stalls.
- Establish the terms of an ongoing relationship.

4. FDAs that will enable you to retain or upgrade your client and advance the relationship . . .

| Serve the Client |
| Advance the Relationship |

- Proactive contact.
- Milestone review meetings.
- Quarterly and annual review meetings.

5. FDAs that enable you to ask each client for introductions and referrals on a timely basis . . .

| New Introductions and Referrals |

- Reviewing your Top 25 clients.
- Focusing on business and life changes.
- Capitalizing on contacts and review meetings.

How to Use the Rainmaker Critical Path System

The *Rainmaker Critical Path System* will help you plan your week so that you spend 70% of your time face-to-face with key clients, qualified affluent prospects, or with people who can introduce or refer you to qualified affluent prospects.

1. Prior to beginning your business activity on Monday morning, list the high-impact **Fixed Daily Activities** (**FDAs**) you plan to DO that week. Include . . .
   - A description of that activity.

Critical Path ORGANIZER Week of __/__/__ to __/__/__

Fixed Daily Activities (FDAs) that place you in *direct contact* with the people who build your business.

FDAs to schedule this week . . .	Purpose	When

Purpose—use one or a combination of the following . . .
+ I & R   + Network   + Alliance   + Client Event   + Follow-Up   + Close Sale   + Retain   + Upgrade

- The **Purpose** of that activity using the guidelines at the bottom of the form.
- **When** that activity will be performed. Include which day or days (plus the time of day, if that's important).

Each week should be planned in advance as much as possible. Add additional FDAs during the week as needed.

2. Go to the **Daily SCHEDULER** page.
   - If you have a daily planner, use the Daily SCHEDULER as a guide for recording that same information in your planner.
   - If you do not have a daily planner, use this Daily SCHEDULER to list Daily Activities and Contacts, and to schedule

Daily SCHEDULER

Day:	**Daily Activites**	
Date:	✓ Business & Personal	

7	
8	
9	
10	
11	
12 Noon	
1	
2	
	Contacts
3	✓ Type F2=Face-to-Face P=Phone E=Email F=Fax
4	
5	
6	
7	

Notes: _____

both appointments and daily activities within specific time
frames to make certain they get done.

Each day should be planned in advance—before you leave the
office each evening.

3. Use the **Prospecting CONTACT Manager** to make certain that
you maintain a *tight line* from one prospect contact to the next.
   - Fill in the name, phone, company, email and address section
   . . . and check **Prospect** at the top.
   - In the **Notes** section, indicate how contact was initiated with
   this prospect: introduced, referred, networking, referral alliance, intimate client event, etc. If introduced or referred, in-

CONTACT Manager

☐ Prospect
☐ Client

Name:		Phone:
Company:	Email:	

Address: _____

City:	State/Prov.	Zip:

Notes . . .

Prospecting—check as completed . . .
___ In Pipeline   ___ First Face-to-Face   ___ Follow-Up Activities   ___ Close the Sale
(Check Client box above)

Contact RESULTS . . .

Date	Purpose & Outcome of Contact	Follow-Up

clude the name of the person who provided that introduction or referral.

- For each contact made, note the **Contact RESULTS** by recording the date, the purpose and outcome of the call, and the specific follow-up that is indicated. Every follow-up should include the type and date.
- Record the follow-up in **Daily SCHEDULER** and file the **CONTACT Manager** alphabetically in a loose-leaf binder until the day before you make the next contact. This will enable you to maintain a *tight line* on this prospect.

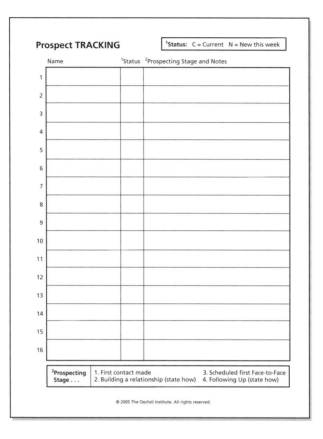

4. Use the **Prospect TRACKING** to keep your pipeline list always in front of you.

   • Write down the **Name** of each prospect that you have qualified, but who hasn't yet become a client.

   • Use the **Status** column to distinguish between current and new prospects.

   • Record the **Prospecting Stage** and any **Notes** you want to remember about each prospect in the last column.

The goal of this system is to keep you on your *Rainmaker Critical Path*, making certain that you spend 70% of your time face-to-face with the people who help you build your business.

About the Author

Matt Oechsli is one of the leading authorities regarding marketing, selling, servicing and developing loyalty with affluent clients. One of the country's busiest and most in-demand sales and business speakers, Mr. Oechsli has authored 11 previous books that include the best sellers *How to Build a 21st Century Financial Practice* and *The Art of Selling to the Affluent.*

With an MBA in Marketing from Anna Maria College in Paxton, MA, a BS from the University of Arizona, certification in clinical hypnotherapy, and working as a counselor of emotionally disturbed youth in New York City—Mr. Oechsli's background is unique, to say the least.

For the past 25 years, Mr. Oechsli has served as the President of the Oechsli Institute in Greensboro, North Carolina, a firm specializing in providing research-based performance improvement programs and tools. He lives in Greensboro, North Carolina with his wife and three children.

Index

12 Commandments of Rainmaking, 144, 145, 146, 147, 148, 149, 150, 151, 152, 153, 154, 155
12-Month Rainmaker Goal, 159, 160, 161, 162, 163, 164, 165, 166

Abraham Lincoln, 9
Achievement Cycle, 50
achievement cycle, 18, 44, 47, 48, 50, 147
Activities, 34, 48, 49, 125
affluence, 2, 45
affluent acquisition targets, 147
affluent business, 36, 60
affluent client, 51, 123, 159
Affluent Client Profile, 72
affluent clientele, 96
affluent clients, 5, 6, 11, 12, 17, 18, 24, 27, 31, 33, 42, 47, 56, 57, 66, 67, 83, 95, 113, 117, 124, 148, 159, 160, 167
affluent consumers, 13, 19, 20, 21, 23, 25, 26, 90, 92, 129, 133, 135
Affluent consumers, 134
affluent markets, 92
affluent prospect, 7, 13, 16, 21, 25, 33, 55, 100, 106, 108, 117, 141, 153, 161
affluent prospects, 8, 12, 13, 14, 18, 25, 36, 51, 60, 66, 68, 69, 70, 79, 93, 100, 102, 128, 129, 135, 150, 160, 161, 162
Albert E. N. Gray, 1, 45
American Bar Association, 137
ANAC Research, 5, 31, 90, 155
ANAC respondents, 51, 57
ANAC Survey, 18, 19, 102
ANAC survey, 105
anchor industry, 79
anomalies, 24
APD Research, 13, 19, 20, 21, 25, 55, 57, 116, 127
APD respondents, 26, 56, 68

Assessment, 33, 43, 99, 100
avoidance behavior, 15, 39, 40
Avoidance Tactics, 35, 43

Be Like Tiger, 154
Be Persistent, 141, 157
Be Seamless, 153

Calvin Coolidge, 125, 151
Cap Gemini report, 58, 59, 69
Caveat Emptor, 25
center-of-influence, 65, 114, 117
centers-of-influence, 18, 58, 65, 66, 68, 69, 73, 98, 102, 117, 126, 138
Chart 1, 6
Chart 2, 32
Chart 3, 33
Chart 4, 57, 58
Chart 5, 61
Chart 6, 99, 100
Chart 7, 105
client satisfaction survey, 126
comfort zone, 2, 12, 18, 33, 40, 44, 45, 46, 48, 50, 117, 154
comfort zones, 16
competencies, 48
Completely Focused, 150
CONTACT Manager, 164, 165
Critical Path, 160, 161, 166
Critical Path System, 160, 162

Daily SCHEDULER, 163, 164, 165
Dale Carnegie, 120
David McCelland, 159
demonstrating, 24, 111
Disco Salesman, 118, 153
Dramatists Guild, 121

elance, 133

emerging affluent, 36
empirical data, 1
experiential learning, 15, 18
Extremely Competitive, 148

financial advisors, 5, 6, 15, 19, 24, 31, 42,
    43, 55, 68, 73, 96, 105, 110, 148
Financial Lord's Prayer, 38
financial professionals, 1, 45, 96, 155
Fixed Daily Activities, 160, 161, 162, 163
Fully Energized, 150

General George C. McClellan, 9
goal accomplishment, 48
goal focus, 18, 45, 46
Google, 114, 128, 130, 131, 135, 150
Google.com, 127, 134, 135
guru, 95, 133

hard chargers, 22
Have Your Antenna Out, 152
high-end service providers, 129
high-impact, 2, 7, 11, 13, 14, 15, 16, 19, 31,
    34, 42, 47, 57, 60, 62, 64, 66, 67, 68, 69,
    70, 87, 88, 97, 99, 101, 102, 106, 107, 113,
    117, 125, 127, 137, 143, 146, 149, 154,
    160, 161, 162
High-Impact Activities, 2, 58, 70
high-impact activities, 2, 7, 11, 16, 31, 34,
    42, 47, 57, 60, 62, 64, 66, 67, 68, 70, 88,
    99, 102, 113, 117, 137
High-impact activities, 88
high-impact activities, 146, 160
high-impact activity, 64, 102, 143, 149
high-impact encounter, 107
high-impact Fixed Daily Activities, 160,
    161, 162
high-impact prospecting, 60
high-impact prospecting activities, 14, 19,
    101, 102, 117, 125, 127, 154
High-impact prospecting FDAs, 161
High-Impact Prospecting Methods, 70
high-impact Rainmaker activities, 7, 13, 87,
    146
high-impact rainmaking activities, 101, 113
highest-impact activities, 13
Highly Disciplined, 149

Ideal Affluent Prospect Profile, 75
Ideal Affluent Targeted Prospect, 84
Ideal Client Profile, 59, 70, 72, 74, 88
industry immersion, 78
internal advocate, 75, 77, 80, 87

Internet, 21, 81, 90, 111, 127, 129, 130, 131,
    134, 135, 150
Internet niche, 129
interpersonal skills, 116, 122, 125
investable assets, 5, 6, 7, 18, 19, 51, 58, 114
investments, 24, 82, 107, 109

John Atkinson, 159
John T. Malloy, 120
Joseph Johnston, 9

key people, 77, 79, 80, 81, 82, 83
Kingpin Rainmaker, 112

Lao Tsu, 136
Life after the Sale, 22
long-term, 7, 12, 56, 84, 87
Love the Game, 154
Low-Impact, 37, 90, 93, 97
low-impact, 37, 43, 90, 97, 101, 102
low-impact activities, 37, 90, 101

mailing lists, 37, 69, 94
Master Rainmaker, 1, 144, 145, 146, 155
Mindset, 2, 9, 10, 31, 32, 33, 34, 40, 42, 43,
    44, 46, 49, 116, 147
Mindset of a Rainmaker, 2, 42, 44
Mindset of a Warrior, 44, 147
moderate-impact activity, 90
My Past Achievements, 48, 49

National Association of Life Underwriters
    Convention, 1
networking, 13, 16, 19, 57, 58, 60, 61, 68
Networking, 34, 58, 61, 71, 74, 90, 161
networking, 70, 74, 81, 82, 88, 89, 100, 107,
    127, 164

Oechsli Institute, 2, 5, 6, 13, 167
outsource, 133

Paul Lemberg, 139
Perks and Pitfalls, 17
personal referrals, 18
Personal Reward, 51
preparation paralysis, 38, 45
Prospect TRACKING, 166
prospecting, 12, 13, 14, 18, 19, 31, 32, 34,
    39, 41, 45, 57, 59, 60, 64, 66, 70, 71, 87,
    88, 90, 97, 101, 102, 117, 125, 127, 152,
    153, 154, 161
prospecting activities, 13, 14, 18, 19, 32, 34,
    45, 57, 66, 97, 101, 102, 117, 125, 127,

154
Prospecting CONTACT Manager, 164
Prospecting Hierarchy, 57
Prospecting Stage, 166
Proving Your Competence, 111

Rainmaker, 1, 2, 5, 6, 7, 8, 10, 11, 12, 13, 14,
   15, 16, 17, 18, 19, 22, 32, 33, 34, 35, 36,
   38, 39, 40, 42, 43, 44, 45, 46, 47, 50, 51,
   60, 62, 63, 64, 66, 67, 70, 78, 87, 88, 91,
   92, 94, 98, 99, 100, 102, 105, 106, 107,
   108, 109, 110, 111, 112, 113, 116, 117,
   118, 119, 120, 123, 124, 125, 134, 136,
   137, 138, 142, 143, 144, 145, 146, 147,
   148, 149, 150, 152, 153, 154, 155, 159,
   160, 162, 166
Rainmaker Activities, 99
Rainmaker Activity & Skills Self-
   Assessment, 100
Rainmaker Antenna, 152
Rainmaker Covenant, 145
Rainmaker creed, 152
Rainmaker Critical Path, 166
Rainmaker Critical Path Activities, 160
Rainmaker Critical Path System, 155, 160,
   162
Rainmaker Game Plan, 34, 43
Rainmaker goals, 147, 148, 155
Rainmaker Institute, 47, 62, 144, 147, 150
Rainmaker Mindset, 29, 33, 40, 46
Rainmaker mindset, 10, 32, 40, 42
Rainmaker Skills, 99
Rainmaker Standard, 159
Rainmaker wannabe, 6, 7, 42, 98, 105, 106,
   117, 149
Rainmaker's Achievement Cycle, 45, 46, 47,
   67, 117, 137, 147, 148, 149, 150, 154
Rainmaker's Rule of Six, 63, 68, 69
Rainmakers, 1, 2, 3, 7, 10, 11, 12, 13, 14, 15,
   16, 17, 18, 22, 25, 39, 40, 47, 50, 62, 64,
   65, 87, 88, 91, 99, 101, 102, 112, 113, 117,
   120, 122, 125, 133, 143, 144, 146, 149,
   150, 151, 152, 153, 154, 155
Rainmakers' Activity Profile, 99
Rainmaking skills, 99, 116, 120, 125, 146,
   148
RAM, 40, 41, 42
RAP, 66, 67
referral alliance, 83, 84, 85, 164
referral-generation skills, 125
referred prospect, 55
René Descartes, 31

Research Facts, 19, 26, 43, 51, 68, 89, 102,
   114, 126, 135, 143, 155
Robert E. Lee, 9

sales skills, 2, 11, 111, 113, 125, 152, 153
Salesman, 35
Seamless Salesperson, 153
Seamless Seller, 118, 119
self-awareness, 40
self-sufficient, 1, 17
selling skills, 15, 16, 36, 125
service professionals, 5, 20, 56
short-term goals, 12
skill coaching, 12
skill session, 62
Skill/Activity Assessment, 99
skills, 2, 7, 10, 11, 12, 16, 17, 18, 19, 21, 32,
   34, 36, 47, 48, 61, 64, 68, 70, 77, 92, 97,
   99, 101, 102, 107, 108, 110, 111, 113, 114,
   116, 117, 120, 122, 125, 126, 146, 148,
   150, 152, 153, 154
statement of intent, 159
statistically significant, 1
strategic alliances, 83, 97, 99
strategic intent, 15, 40, 117
strategic referral alliance, 83, 84, 85
Strategic Referral Alliances, 71, 83

TAKING ACTION, 19, 26, 43, 51, 69, 89,
   102, 114, 126, 135, 143, 155
targeted networking, 13, 60, 127
targeted prospect, 34, 73
targeted prospects, 34, 93
The McClellan Mindset, 9
The Right Activities, 13
The Right Mindset, 10
The Right Skills, 15, 103
Tiger Woods, 10, 11, 113, 147, 154
Toastmasters, 120
Top 25 Introduction Book, 63, 64, 68, 69
Top 25 Introduction Notebook, 63, 64, 73,
   89, 127, 135
Totally Goal Driven, 147

Value Trumps Price, 24

wealthy consumers, 20
work without a net, 10, 12

Yahoo, 128, 130, 131
Yogi Berra, 147